S0-ASI-547

# Praise for
## *A Significant Life*

"There is a life beyond the one we know. Our souls yearn for it, our dreams are filled with it, and our hopes reach for it in the lives of others. It is the life of meaning we were made to live, the one fueled by the power of a destiny to fulfill. Jim Graff has charted the pathway to that life. *A Significant Life* is a stirring call to the highlands of God's best for our lives."

—STEPHEN MANSFIELD, author of *The Faith of George W. Bush*
and *The Faith of the American Soldier*

"*A Significant Life* does a beautiful job instructing the reader how to live with meaning and purpose. This book is filled with rich, solid nuggets of truth. I encourage you to take some time and follow along as Jim Graff takes you on a journey to discover your own unique significance. This book is exactly what you need."

—NICKY CRUZ, founder of Nicky Cruz Outreach
and author of *Soul Obsession* and *One Holy Fire*

"In *A Significant Life*, Jim Graff eloquently unfolds a strategy he and other great leaders are using to spark revolutions for Christ in small towns, counties, and all areas of America. His concept and example give hope and inspiration that every church in every community can be part of rescuing our country."

—RON LUCE, president and founder of Teen Mania Ministries,
and author of *Battle Cry for a Generation* and *Revolution YM*

"*A Significant Life* is a wonderful book about the importance of being obedient to God and being in his perfect will for your life, no matter how large or small your church may be. Everyone is significant in the body of Christ, and everyone has been given an assignment. This book will help you understand that when you live out your purpose, God is so proud of you. Similarly, I am proud of Jim. He is a great son-in-law, and I salute him for writing this book."

—DODIE OSTEEN, cofounder of Lakewood Church

"Has self-doubt or the challenges of others caused you to question what dwells in the recesses of your heart—God's vision and purpose for you? *A Significant Life* lays all the cards on the table. Pastor Jim Graff dissects the stumbling blocks and obstacles that can easily discourage us, and he brings us into a place where we can see all the resources that are before us. You will finish this book knowing that you can achieve all that God has entrusted to you."

—BILL WILSON, senior pastor and founder of Metro Ministries, and author of *Christianity in the Crosshairs*

"*A Significant Life* speaks directly to the age-old question of humanity: *Why am I here?* Through a revealing dissection of King David's life, Jim Graff leads us on an exciting journey of discovery and reawakening of our God-given dreams and callings. Each page feels like a breath of fresh air for people who are beaten down, weary, or needing direction for their lives. With a pastor's heart, Jim encourages us to throw off all the entanglements in our lives and gain the confidence in God to live the lives we were created for."

—JOHN AND LISA BEVERE, authors and speakers, Messenger International

"Whether your years on earth have been blessed like Jacob's or have left you feeling more like Esau—red, hairy, and gruff with good reason—the principles explored in *A Significant Life* will help you live a life that has a lasting impact on the world. Jim Graff gives a profound teaching on fulfilling the calling God has for each and every one of us."

—TED HAGGARD, pastor and author of *Foolish No More!* *The Jerusalem Diet,* and *From This Day Forward*

# A
## *Significant*
# LIFE

# JIM GRAFF

FOREWORD BY
## JOEL OSTEEN

# A *Significant* LIFE

## FULFILLING YOUR ETERNAL
## POTENTIAL EVERY DAY

### WATERBROOK
PRESS

A SIGNIFICANT LIFE
PUBLISHED BY WATERBROOK PRESS
12265 Oracle Boulevard, Suite 200
Colorado Springs, Colorado 80921
*A division of Random House Inc.*

All Scripture quotations, unless otherwise indicated, are taken from the Holy Bible, New International Version®. NIV®. Copyright © 1973, 1978, 1984 by International Bible Society. Used by permission of Zondervan Publishing House. All rights reserved. Scripture quotations marked (MSG) are taken from The Message by Eugene H. Peterson. Copyright © 1993, 1994, 1995, 1996, 2000, 2001, 2002. Used by permission of NavPress Publishing Group. All rights reserved. Scripture quotations marked (NASB) are take from the New American Standard Bible®. © Copyright The Lockman Foundation 1960, 1962, 1963, 1968, 1971, 1972, 1973, 1975, 1977, 1995. Used by permission. (www.Lockman.org). Scripture quotations marked (NKJV) are taken from the New King James Version®. Copyright © 1982 by Thomas Nelson Inc. Used by permission. All rights reserved. Scripture quotations marked (Phillips) are taken from The New Testament in Modern English, Revised Edition © 1972 by J. B. Phillips. Copyright renewed © 1986, 1988 by Vera M. Phillips.

Italics in Scripture quotations reflect the author's added emphasis.

Details in some anecdotes and stories have been changed to protect the identities of the persons involved.

10-Digit ISBN 1-4000-7262-X
13-Digit ISBN 978-1-4000-7262-0

Copyright © 2006 by Jim Graff

All rights reserved. No part of this book may be reproduced or transmitted in any form or by any means, electronic or mechanical, including photocopying and recording, or by any information storage and retrieval system, without permission in writing from the publisher.

WATERBROOK and its deer design logo are registered trademarks of WaterBrook Press, a division of Random House Inc.

Library of Congress Cataloging-in-Publication Data
Graff, Jim.
    A significant life : fulfilling your eternal potential every day / Jim Graff ; foreword by Joel Osteen. — 1st ed.
        p. cm.
    ISBN-13: 978-1-4000-7262-0
  1. Christian life.  I. Title.
    BV4501.3.G69 2006
    248.4—dc22

                                             2006020853

Printed in the United States of America
2006—First Edition

10  9  8  7  6  5  4  3  2  1

~

*I dedicate this book to:*

My father, Ken Graff Sr. (1928–1985), a dedicated researcher at PPG Industries by day and a community volunteer firefighter, an ambulance driver, a Little League coach, and a devoted husband and father by night. To my best friend, the man who taught me to believe in myself and my God-given potential, my prayer is that more homes would be filled with fathers like you.

My father-in-law for thirteen years, Pastor John Osteen (1921–1999), my mentor in ministry who showed me that buildings don't need pastors but that people do. An encouraging and compassionate leader, this man taught me to believe in others and their God-given potential. I pray more churches would be filled with pastors like you.

Every pastor laboring in America's smaller counties and in overlooked places of the world. My prayer is that you would flourish and abound in the place of significance God has called you to.

# Contents

# PART IV: COOPERATION

# PART V: COMMUNITY

# Foreword

E ach day we can easily become consumed by the details of life: running errands, preparing meals, chauffeuring children, paying bills, and working overtime. It's sometimes hard to remember why we do what we do—the deeper design behind the details, the motivation beyond surviving another day. It reminds me of walking through a forest so overgrown that blazing the trail seems to become more important than where it leads us. On this kind of hike, it's not hard to lose motivation for the journey.

If I asked you what matters most to you on this journey, my guess is that you'd respond like many of us: God, family, friends, church, work. *But if I asked you if you're living a significant life, how would you respond?* As you drive your kids to school or commute to work, pay the bills and shop for groceries, it may not feel particularly momentous, even though they're all part of every day. But beneath the surface, don't you know God created you for more? Day in and day out, do you seek a meaningful life, full of God-given passionate purpose?

This question is certainly not new. In his letter to the Corinthians, Paul reminds us all to stay focused on the finish line, not on the speed bumps we encounter along the way: "Do you not know that in a race all the runners run, but only one gets the prize? Run in such a way as to get the prize" (1 Corinthians 9:24). In order to capture the rewarding life we were created to live, we must keep our eyes on the prize. We do this by focusing on our God-given purposes. We do this by living each day with an awareness of its eternal significance.

Like cold water to a weary runner, *A Significant Life* will refresh your spirit as you seek to make every day count. Whether you're already living with a sense of significance or struggling to discover what is truly meaningful, the powerful message contained in this book will inspire you. I've known my brother-in-law Jim Graff for more than twenty years, and he is like a brother to me. He has a passion for empowering individuals, churches, and communities to discover their significance. Jim clearly has a message that the Lord has burned in his heart, one that is relevant, meaningful, and life-changing.

Jim loves helping people find their unique significance, so they can unleash it toward eternal goals. He understands the ways our human nature and media-saturated culture pressure us to compare ourselves with others, making us feel like we come up short. In *A Significant Life,* Jim helps us move beyond a bigger-is-always-better mind-set and discover the soul satisfaction that can only come from living out of our true identities as image-bearers of God. With biblical insight and personal examples, Jim will inspire you to explore your life in profound ways as he guides you through five key areas necessary to developing your personal significance.

Life can be challenging as we encounter painful trials and inevitable disappointments. But with our faith firmly rooted in God and our identity grounded in the special purpose for which he created us, we can experience a level of joy and peace that the world can never give us. If you want to fulfill the eternal potential for which you were created, then read this book. If you need encouragement to continue the journey of purposeful living, then Jim's message will uplift you. It's my firm belief that you will be forever changed as you embrace what it means to enjoy a significant life!

—Joel Osteen

# Acknowledgments

For the many people who have been a part of my life and who have made a contribution to this project, I want to extend my sincere thanks and heartfelt gratitude. Thank you to:

Dudley Delffs, a talented editor and friend who made this project such a pleasant one.

WaterBrook staff, a joy to work with, for believing in me and in the overlooked people and places.

Tom Winters, for helping to make this project a reality.

David Swann, Duane Sheriff, Mike Connaway, Mike Ewoldt, Mark Harrell, Pat Butcher—pastors and partners who have shared the vision and labored earnestly with me to establish the Significant Church Network.

Rob Koke and Tom Newman—God-given friends who have been a constant source of encouragement and strength to me these past twenty years.

My staff at Faith Family Church, for your continued love and dedication to God's work. It's a joy to carry out God's purposes with you.

Faith Family Church. Any pastor would be blessed to have you as a flock. Thank you for your love, prayers, and faithful partnership these past seventeen years. You're the best.

My mother-in-law, Dodie Osteen, and to the Osteen family, for being great examples in both life and ministry.

My mother, Jean Graff (1932–1985), and my big brother, Ken Graff (1955–1994), for nurturing dreams in me because you cared.

My three sisters, Karen, Sharon, and Linda, for filling my life with special memories and constant love and support.

My children—Michael, Andrea, Emily, and Geoffrey—my special rewards. The joy you've brought into my life has superseded my highest dreams.

My wife, Tamara, the woman of my dreams and the best friend I've ever had. You make every aspect of life so much more wonderful.

# INTRODUCTION

# Is Bigger Always Better?

In the early 1990s my life was in crisis, but not the kind of crisis easily understood by most people. At the time, I had been serving Faith Family Church in Victoria, Texas, for several years, and the Lord had blessed it. In just a few years, the church grew from two hundred fifty to several hundred more members. Like so many of us, whether in the ministry or the corporate culture, I had been conditioned to believe bigger was always better, so our increase in size meant success. Or did it?

Coming out of college, I wasn't sure if God was calling me to full-time ministry. So I went on the mission field and preached throughout Africa and Europe. When I returned, I sensed the Lord leading me into pastoral ministry, and I was encouraged in this pursuit by trusted friends and family members. Not long after that God called me to Faith Family Church, which is in a small community in southeast Texas. Having grown up in a rural Pennsylvania community, I found the church to be a perfect fit since I never wanted to lose that small-town feel of community.

The problem, though, was that most of my peers were serving in mega-churches that boast thousands of members. With only hundreds attending Faith Family at the time, the difference between the numbers felt a little bit like failure. I needed to be moving toward a bigger and better church to pastor, right? Wasn't that how I would know I was doing a good job? Don't most of us, regardless of profession, mark our success by increasing our numbers?

Then my chance came. In 1993, a pastor and friend of my father-in-law came to me and said, "Jim, I'm ready to hand over my life's work. I'd like you to consider taking over my church." Let me tell you, this church was every pastor's dream: about two thousand active members, a large staff, financial stability, and more ministries than I could imagine. By the grace of God, this was my opportunity. Now I could have what I thought I wanted. So—certain I would say yes—I went to Arlington, Texas, but I left feeling that something just wasn't right. I didn't understand, though, what it could be.

## FOOTBALL FIELDS AND FAITH

I knew God had a plan for my life, that he had called me, raised me up in ministry, led me to the mission field, and given me early success that enabled greater opportunity. And now this move to Arlington was the next logical step...right? But something nagged at my heart, and to tell the truth, I was a little disappointed in myself for not jumping on the opportunity. I wanted my life to be like King David's, whose life we'll study in this book and whose godly leadership affected his generation in significant ways. So I wondered why I couldn't get on board. I've come to believe, in the time since, that pastors, along with most of us, fight a battle between wanting versus having, and I just wasn't sure that what I had at the time (a smaller church) was what I wanted. But truth be told, even after I found myself smack-dab in the middle of an opportunity to have what I thought I wanted (a megachurch), I still wasn't satisfied.

When I got back to Victoria, my brother-in-law invited me on a hunting trip in Arkansas, and it sounded like a great diversion. Driving north out of Texas, I received a glimpse into my discontent. As I passed through small town after small town, I discovered a truth about my dilemma in the high-school football stadiums along the roadside. Any of you who have seen *Friday Night Lights* know what football is to Texans. We love our football, and we support it with everything we've got. In almost every Texas community I passed, a stadium sat in the middle of town as a shrine to our love affair with football. But as I drove through those small towns, I noticed that those great football stadiums—built with the finest materials and engineering skills available—were sitting in the middle of communities filled with struggling churches. God used that observation to help me understand my heart.

Those churches symbolized a different side of church life and made me realize why I needed to stay at Faith Family. Those churches were guided by pastors and church leaders who had an important task to do. Their churches would probably never reach the size of many big-city churches, but they certainly had their own unique significance. If they embraced their roles, they could affect in very meaningful ways higher percentages of the people in their towns than most big-city churches ever would.

Then I realized something about myself: my upbringing in rural Pennsylvania, my love of small communities, my uneasiness about big cities—that's how God made me. Those traits pointed to his purpose for me, and now I had a chance to use my gifts to enrich my smaller church as well as other smaller churches and even individuals who might be struggling with whether bigger is always better.

Not long after I came home from that trip, I called my staff together. On the local front, I had always said, "I want Faith Family to be a place my friends would go." Not just my Christian friends, but those friends who I knew needed a loving place to learn about God. I wanted my church to accept the people of our local community; if people felt accepted, they would eventually ask the reason for our faith and, hopefully, join us at our church.

So I asked my church to dream about a diverse staff touching the people of our area through various gifts and interests. I wanted them to go beyond thinking of our individual talents alone and start focusing on our collective abilities and how together we could reflect Christ in our town. In short, I felt God was calling me to make Faith Family Church a significant influence in our community, no matter what our size.

On a larger scale, my heart turned to overlooked people in America and around the world. With just a little research, I quickly learned that ninety million people live in America's smaller cities and towns. If those ninety million were considered their own nation, they would be the thirteenth largest country on the planet. That is definitely significant!

I guessed that we'd find some heroic believers laboring faithfully in those smaller churches, and we did. But I also wondered if we would find additional smaller cities and towns with an even greater need for ministry. And we definitely did! Those discoveries made me start thinking about significance even more deeply, and I have come to realize since then that *where significance is undiscovered, potential stays undeveloped.* That's why those churches needed to know they were vital to God's plan. Over 80 percent of our churches in America have fewer than two hundred people in them. What will happen in our country if they lose heart? Less than 2 percent of Americans attend megachurches, which means that the majority of American Christians are being discipled in much-needed smaller churches that must prosper if we are to fulfill what's on God's heart. We at Faith Family Church went to work dreaming on their behalf.

## SMALLER TOWNS, BIGGER IMPACT

The movement took shape in 2000 when we surveyed pastors in over two thousand counties across America. While our ultimate vision is to help plant significant faith communities in every overlooked village in the world, we started with the United States, and our goal was simple: discover the state of the church in small-county American life and figure out how to strengthen it.

And 2000 was a strange year. Remember the "red" states that threw the presidential election into a frenzy? Remember the national news media calling the Bush-Gore election in the early evening and then having to retract their announcements later that night? In the year we decided to figure out what was going on in small-town America, small-town America was putting itself back on the social and political map. To us at Faith Family, the election spoke of the significance of this community's voice, of the potential that was ready to be unleashed for God's kingdom.

The survey revealed more than we bargained for, and it brought me into partnership with incredible pastors and church leaders doing impressive works largely unheard of. The survey also showed us that people everywhere, particularly in the rural areas and small counties of our country, long to know that who they are counts and what they do matters. It's not just pastors and those in full-time ministry who long to know that what they spend their lives doing is worthwhile.

This is the good news: we are *all* longing to make a difference, in our families, in our jobs, in our places of worship, in our neighborhoods, in all the places where we live life. And this is the even better news: we *can* make a significant difference. Like King David centuries ago, we can change the world we live in—that's what the survey conveyed to us. We saw in black and white that all those who honor God by reflecting his image and living out who he made them can be people of impact. Living a significant life is not just about building bigger churches or raising more dollars or increasing membership. It's about becoming all God truly created us to be and living fully in his image as his children. That is when we discover our potential and live out our purpose.

Perhaps you're feeling skeptical at this point. "That's all fine and good, Jim," you say, "but my faith is a little shaky right now, and life really isn't so great. You pastors out there can find your significance, but I live in the real world." My friend, you are exactly the person I'm writing to even as I'm writing to ministers who may have already glimpsed their significance. All of us need to realize that we don't have to live a large life in the glare of a media spotlight to be important. We don't have to be wealthy, dressed in the right designer duds, or driving the latest SUV to matter. We don't need a title, an advanced degree, or an invitation to the White House. This book is written for people like you who want to make your relationships meaningful, who want to live happy and satisfied as you invest your life, and who believe that God has ordained us to live—one day at a time—lives of purpose and meaning. This is not a book of promises or formulas; it's a book designed to help you explore your potential and honor your significance.

So where do we begin? Well, once a year at our church, we get together and dream. Our starting point for dreaming can be found in Ephesians: "Now to him who is able to do immeasurably more than all we ask or imagine, according to his power that is at work within us, to him be glory in the church and in Christ Jesus throughout all generations, for ever and ever!" (3:20–21).

We want people to see God at work in a special way, and we know the Bible clearly points out how this happens. We want to unleash God's power to "do immeasurably more than all we ask or imagine" as he faithfully leads and guides us. We believe that history has confirmed what we believe to be true, and every year the group reminds me that we're to be pursuing dreams that require us to work together with God.

## Eternal Significance Today

So where do we begin in our efforts to find our true significance, to live meaningful lives that fulfill our eternal potential every day? I believe that this fruit of significance begins with the seeds of hope that God placed within us all. Like David, we begin by tending those seeds—or Cs, as I like to call them—and cultivating them in five key areas: developing *confidence,* being a person of *character, concentrating* on God's will, *cooperating* with God (and others) in carrying out his plans, and participating in *community.*

So join me on an exciting journey of discovery and personal growth as we examine what it means to live the life for which God has created you.

We'll learn from the examples of some remarkably significant people, some famous and some you may never have heard of, some from the Bible and some from everyday life. Together we'll discover what it means to live out eternity in real time, fulfilling our divine potential every day in ways that change our own lives as well as the lives of those around us.

Turn the page and take that first step toward being who you were meant to be, a special someone living a significant life.

# PART I

# Confidence

*But I trust in your unfailing love;*
*my heart rejoices in your salvation.*
*I will sing to the LORD,*
*for he has been good to me.*

PSALM 13:5–6

# CHAPTER 1

# The Confidence to Dream

As a pastor I'm often privileged to be in the room as someone passes from this life to the next. I've shared in this intimate moment with the old as well as with those we would consider too young to die, with both men and women, with those leaving behind million-dollar estates as well as those just barely getting by financially. In each case my experience has verified the saying that people on their deathbeds don't wish they had worked more hours at the office. However, my encounter with one older gentleman, a man I'll call Bill, made me think more deeply about this truth.

Bill had led a life all of us who knew him would consider significant. A lifelong Christian, he was a faithful husband of forty years, a devoted father and grandfather, a successful businessman, and a leader in our community. Yet as cancer ravaged his body, Bill began questioning what he had done with his life and the choices he had made along the way. During one of our conversations near the end, Bill told me, "I certainly don't wish that I'd worked more in this lifetime. But I do wish I'd had the confidence to work more toward the things that matter."

I asked him to explain. "Jim," he said, "when I grew up, there was a lot of uncertainty in the world. There wasn't the freedom to discover who you were and what you wanted to do. You did what was needed, what was expected." Bill went on to describe his passion for baseball, something we shared, and how his father had squelched his dream of playing professionally. "It would have been okay if I'd never made the big leagues," he concluded. "It's just that I wish I'd had the confidence to try." He paused for a moment before adding, "If I've done one thing for my children and grandchildren, I hope it's been to create confidence in them so that they're willing to take risks."

My encounter with Bill left me thinking about my own boyhood and the ways my parents encouraged me and allowed me to take risks. And I certainly left with the same conviction as Bill, hoping that I ignite in my children the same kind of confidence, the kind of spark that's needed to fuel their dreams. It also forced me to consider the role that confidence plays in living a significant life.

## COUNTERFEIT CONFIDENCE

You might not expect our exploration of significant living to begin with the topic of confidence, a quality that usually accumulates through experience and might therefore seem more appropriate to examine later in the book. But as I've interacted with numerous individuals over the years, they tell me that what most often keeps them from living a more meaningful life is lack of confidence.

As I thought about how this barrier hinders people, the phrase *con man* came to mind. Con men (or women) have so much confidence in their acting abilities that they try to trick people into handing over money—and they too often succeed. They use their counterfeit confidence to acquire selfish, unethical, and usually illegal gains rather than to achieve God-given goals of significance. How much greater, then, should our confidence be when we're pursuing higher goals? Shouldn't we be more confident than even the best con men and women? Why, then, does genuine confidence seem in short supply?

Many people have told me they can often picture themselves living more authentic, more fulfilling lives, but that the steps necessary to get there just seem too hard. Or they're not sure exactly how to move toward what they can only glimpse in their minds. Or they're afraid that the significant lives they imagine for themselves are not what God wants for them.

Regardless of the specifics of their struggles, many people clearly feel that they lack what it takes to risk their safety and fully embrace who God made them to be. That's why I believe that in order to move toward living our most significant lives, we must fan back into flames the embers of dreams we've let cool over the years. Perhaps when we were younger, we found it easier to see ourselves achieving great goals and feeling successful about who we would become. Yet as day-to-day life—the bills to pay and kids to raise, the demands of our jobs and the responsibilities of caring for those we love—wears on us, we find it difficult to believe that the process matters as much as the destination that seems so out of reach.

So how do we move from where we are right now toward what we know we were made for, toward those dreams of our best lives? I'm convinced that confidence is a crucial cornerstone, and therefore a good starting point, in the building of a significant life. Confidence is foundational in several ways, particularly in how it connects us to God and to other people, the two lifelines of significant living.

Confidence and the dreams that fuel it can sustain our faith when obstacles seem to close in around us. And divine confidence—from knowing God—reminds us that more is going on in our lives than meets the eye. God has an incredible plan for us and wants us to move boldly into the unique design of who he made us to be. When life seems hard and we're struggling, confidence in more than just ourselves helps us persevere. Similarly, the people around us who form our community also shape our confidence by reminding us who we are and how we work together to accomplish goals larger than any one of us could achieve alone.

In fact, this message forms the heart of what this book is all about: *when we fully accept how God made us and pursue within our community the purposes that he sets before us, then our lives become more fulfilling.* Any questions and regrets we have about how to spend our lives each day fade as we glimpse the eternal differences we're making. So there may not be a better place to begin our quest for meaningful lives than by examining the way our dreams and the dreams of others fuel our journeys of significance.

## DREAM A LITTLE DREAM

In our twenty-first-century entrepreneurial culture, we're often encouraged to dream big. Living the American Dream seems to be about pulling yourself up by your bootstraps, succeeding by your own abilities, and then basking in newfound affluence. In many ways our country was built by this kind of work ethic, and taking responsibility for achieving our goals is essential to fulfilling them. However, I wonder if by focusing only on the fulfillment of our individual dreams we aren't missing out on something more significant. You see, I believe that God-given dreams are meant to be shared and that they are intended to bring glory to God's kingdom and abundance to the people around us. As we will see, in Scripture we see this truth demonstrated time and time again.

I've also noticed, in my own experience and in the lives of others, that dreams must start small before they can "grow up" into larger dreams. In fact, before you and I can feel confident enough to move forward in the direction of our dreams, first we must learn how to distinguish a true dream from a passing fancy or a fantasy wish. It's one thing for me to have the desire of playing in the World Series; it's another for me to see that desire grow into a calling and then into a fulfilling dream shared by others.

We must also learn to distinguish a selfish dream from a God-given dream. How do we know when our dream is truly in accordance with our Father's will? How do we separate a passing daydream from a dream that has eternal significance—and needs to be acted upon?

Perhaps a good place to begin exploring this question is the early Christian church and Peter's sermon at Pentecost. In Acts 2:17, Peter quoted the Old Testament book of Joel:

> In the last days, God says,
> I will pour out my Spirit on all people.
> Your sons and daughters will prophesy,
> your young men will see visions,
> your old men will dream dreams.

Before we consider what this message meant, it seems important to remember who's speaking. As you may recall, Peter denied knowing Jesus just hours before the Crucifixion. And now Peter finds himself preaching to other followers of Christ! His turnaround certainly reminds us that, even when we stray from our God-given purposes, it's never too late for us to return to our dreams. Peter likely had some doubts about his place in this group and probably wondered if others were willing to trust him. But on this important occasion when the Holy Spirit descended at Pentecost, Peter spoke confidently, and he led the church into a new era of empowerment.

Now let's look at Peter's message that in the last days young men will have visions while old men will dream dreams. The distinction Peter makes between the two emphasizes an important difference for us. I believe that, in this context, a vision is something that individuals imagine for their own lives. A vision is something they have the strength to pursue, the energy to fulfill, and the time to invest in. On the other hand, this passage implies that dreams are something we share within a network of other people's lives.

Visions and dreams work together, in the same way individuals unite to form communities that can fulfill what may appear to be a person's impossible dream. One reason I love this scripture is because it so clearly highlights the significance of both the young and the old in our communities. In our culture we too often overlook our elderly. We sometimes view them as living beyond their usefulness and out of touch with our present reality. This scripture highlights an important role the elderly can play in a healthy community.

This scripture tells us of old men who even in the latter years of life have not turned off their dream machines. They don't view their role in society as over or their lives as faded or insignificant. Instead, this passage describes a generation that realize their significance. They may not have the time, resources, or strength to carry out the dreams they hold, but they continue to dream of a better tomorrow. They also know that by instilling those dreams in the hearts and minds of a younger generation, they not only fulfill their own personal significance, but they also pass on seeds of significance and confidence to a younger generation. Those inherited dreams become visions for people who do have the time, strength, and resources to make the dreams reality. Proverbs repeatedly reminds the young to listen to the words of the wise and gain wisdom. There is nothing like the encouragement of experience and wisdom to birth confidence in younger hearts.

## Making a You-Turn

Perhaps another example will make this distinction between personal visions and corporate dreams even clearer. As I mentioned in the introduction, I'd like to use David as an example of a godly and significant life not because he was perfect but because he was so human. He loved God and longed to serve him even as he struggled with his own weaknesses, failures, and sin. David is also well suited for our purposes because Scripture gives us his story in great detail. We see in the life of David a man pursuing his God-given purpose in community—and struggling along the way.

As we'll explore, David's confidence was ignited in some rather unique ways, including through the dreams of his elders. Consider, for instance, the way the prophet Samuel's choice of David as the next king was God's way of validating his calling on his chosen young man. The story begins with David's predecessor, King Saul, falling into disfavor with God because of his disobedient attitude. Consequently, Saul lost his God-given fire and purpose and so God had to correct him. He did so through the words of Samuel, the very man God had used to anoint Saul king. This time, however, Samuel's words forced Saul to confront his flaws and realize that he would be replaced as God's chosen leader.

Samuel felt grieved that he had to rebuke a great man about his failings. However, he also experienced an incredible excitement as he participated in the anointing of a younger man, a shepherd from the backwoods town of Bethlehem. In Samuel's anointing—the sign of God's selection of him as the next king—David received affirmation that sparked a vision in his heart. Because of that vision, Israel's tribes were reunited and the nation underwent a spiritual awakening. Through David and his descendants, God accomplished far more than all the old men in Israel ever dreamed.

But Samuel, David, and those around them in this story couldn't see all that awaited them as they wrestled with this change of events. Scripture makes it clear that Samuel struggled with his assignment to rebuke Saul. Perhaps Samuel felt somehow responsible since he had anointed Saul in the first place. Furthermore, Samuel may have felt too invested in Saul's rule to anticipate what God had in store next. Maybe he even blamed God for instructing him to choose someone God knew would eventually fail. Regardless of the reasons for Samuel's mixed emotions, God didn't allow Samuel's sorrow to steal his future:

> How long will you mourn for Saul, since I have rejected him
> as king over Israel? Fill your horn with oil and be on your
> way; I am sending you to Jesse of Bethlehem. I have chosen
> one of his sons to be king. (1 Samuel 16:1)

I can't help but think that God's words here have great relevance for our lives' transitions as we move from past sorrow toward future joy. For many of us, this "you-turn" is often the starting point for pursuing a more significant life. We have to get around the corners of our pasts, including our disappointments and failures, in order to move into the opportunities of the future.

Too often, however, it's tempting to mourn far more than our losses merit, and we end up sinking into self-pity. Now I'm not saying that Samuel did this. I'm only pointing out that after a major disappointment in life, it's tough to anticipate any good things ahead. I'm also not downplaying the importance of grief, which we, in our hyperfast culture, often struggle to own. But even when our grief is real and necessary, God won't allow us to grieve ourselves right out of his blessings. Just because one marriage fails, not all marriages will. Just because we argue with our kids doesn't mean that we have terrible relationships with them. Just because a business struggles through a hard season of drought doesn't mean that it can't eventually bloom into new fruitfulness.

When present disappointments block or distort our view of the future, however, the ripple effect is real. People around us focus on their own disappointments and failures as well. And because we're stuck, we can't envision where God is taking us or how he wants to use us—and because those around us are stuck as well, they don't have dreams to share with us. When we're stuck like this, simply managing our failures in life seems much easier than risking failure in an attempt to fulfill a dream. However, when we let go of our disappointments and move through our grief rather than cling to it, we become open to new dreams. We can then share our dreams and pass them on to those around us.

## GOD'S AFFIRMATION

I'll never forget how I experienced this firsthand. Not long after I returned from my Arkansas hunting trip and my congregation partnered with me in casting a vision for the smaller churches across America, a great man of God named TL Osborn came to our church. For those of you who don't know, Osborn is an evangelist who has spoken all over the world. Only Billy Graham has probably spoken in person to more people in his generation.

After church that particular Sunday, Reverend Osborn came to my office, and the fire and passion in his eyes consumed me to the point that I was almost afraid. He knew of our vision for smaller churches in overlooked places and the work we were doing to honor them. "Jim," he said, "this vision is the most exciting thing that I've heard about in a long, long time. Churches like this are starting to take hold in the nations of the world. Smaller counties are desolate and needy, and you must keep this thing moving."

Wow, was he kidding? Right after God gave me this dream, he confirmed it by bringing into my office one of the most notable spokespersons of his kingdom. How much more affirmation could I ask for than this vote of confidence from someone who knew what was happening in smaller churches around the world? Furthermore, when a person of stature reaches into the lives of small people, small people feel tall. That's why godly leaders like Samuel must keep their eyes focused on God-given dreams. Their affirmations of such dreams spark confidence in the hearts of the people around them.

Let me tell you, when Reverend Osborn came into my life, I trusted him not only because he was a man of stature, but because this man of stature spoke to my small vision. Through his confirmation, God affirmed our plan. I recognized that our dream—and it truly seemed like a dream because it was so much bigger than what we ourselves could accomplish—was of God and that we were moving in the right direction.

So often our confidence falters when we start into the difficult daily grind needed to turn a dream into reality. We find ourselves preoccupied among the trees and lose sight of the forest through which we're blazing a trail. But if we look to the Lord for his guidance and commit our dreams to him, then we can expect him to affirm what he has started. As Scripture reminds us, "He who began a good work in you will carry it on to completion until the day of Christ Jesus" (Philippians 1:6).

## NEW INVESTMENTS

As God keeps us from getting mired in our pasts, he points us toward new investments that will yield his fruit when it's time. This shouldn't surprise us. It seems basic that if we're preoccupied with old matters, we can't seize new opportunities. Embracing this truth is crucial as we move forward into more significant living, and we see this truth reinforced in the process of Samuel's selection of David. Just after asking Samuel how long he will mourn over Saul, God tells him it's time to get back to work:

> Take a heifer with you, and say, "I have come to sacrifice
> to the LORD." Invite Jesse to the sacrifice, and I will show
> you what to do. You are to anoint for me the one I indicate.
> (1 Samuel 16:2)

Clearly, that was the time for Samuel to get on with the things of God. Self-pity and introspection can be dream thieves. Sometimes the deeper we go inside, the more we lose sight of how God-directed actions can change the outside. That's why, every day, we need to come into God's presence and acknowledge our need for his mercy and forgiveness, for his direction and guidance. We must own our failures in order to let go of them before him. That's what God's instructions to Samuel were all about: in that time, personal sins were forgiven and then forgotten through a blood sacrifice. This process of confessing and of embracing God's grace frees us up to receive the blessings ahead.

But after we're forgiven, our focus should move away from the past and toward the way our present actions will affect the future. To continue walking around singing the same old sad, self-pitying tunes in our minds can be so tempting. Instead, we should be making efforts to move on. Just as Samuel obediently filled his horn with oil and took a heifer to sacrifice, we must move beyond our past failures and fight for what matters most in our hearts. We all have work to do, and there is no time to keep running through our old accounts. Investing in a life of purpose pays far more dividends.

## INSIDE OUT

Finally, God created confidence in Samuel by having him focus on God's promises instead of on apparent problems. As the prophet anticipated selecting the new king, for instance, his expectations conflicted with God's criteria for the new leader. Directed to Jesse's house in Bethlehem, Samuel probably assumed that the new king would stand out from all others in the household. Perhaps to counter this mind-set, the Lord said the following to Samuel as Jesse's sons were assembling:

> Do not consider his appearance or his height, for I have
> rejected him. The LORD does not look at the things man
> looks at. Man looks at the outward appearance, but the
> LORD looks at the heart. (1 Samuel 16:7)

It may seem curious to us that God instructed Samuel to ignore the physical qualities that might have made for a good king (after all, the king needed to be a strong leader and fierce warrior). But it's clear once again that God looks at things differently than you or I do. As Jesse's sons paraded in front of Samuel, the prophet heard that message reinforced over and over. Logically, it would have made sense for the oldest son, Eliab, to be the chosen one. So even after God had instructed Samuel ahead of time on his criteria for a king, the prophet still thought he had the selection figured out. Eliab stepped forward, and Samuel thought he must be the one. Tall (like Saul), dark-skinned (like Saul), and handsome (like Saul), Eliab basically looked like a king, which was exactly how the people of Israel chose their kings—with human eyes.

But God was looking for his leader from the inside out, not the other way around, and he made it clear to Samuel that Eliab was not his choice. So Samuel considered more of Jesse's sons, and God's response was always similar:

> Jesse had seven of his sons pass before Samuel, but Samuel said to him, "The LORD has not chosen these." So he asked Jesse, "Are these all the sons you have?"
>
> "There is still the youngest," Jesse answered, "but he is tending the sheep."
>
> Samuel said, "Send for him; we will not sit down until he arrives." (1 Samuel 16:10–11)

When this young man, really no more than a boy, arrived, Samuel realized that David was the one. As unlikely as it seemed for the youngest, the weakest, the one the others had dismissed, to be God's choice, Samuel knew enough about the way God works to see that he'd finally found the nation's next king. Samuel had to lay aside his expectations and any criteria he might've used to select the king and so remain faithful to God's direction, as surprising or unlikely as the divine instructions might have seemed. Thankfully for Israel, Samuel said yes to God, but I'm guessing not without some head-scratching as he wondered what God was up to. Samuel was forced to pursue the dream given by God, not one focused on himself or one imagined by other people.

## GROWING UP

Following Samuel's example, you and I must make sure that we are connected with the visions and dreams God has for us and not ones we manufacture to promote our own agendas. I'm convinced that the confidence we have from God keeps us growing upward, toward higher achievements, bigger dreams, and more-fulfilling relationships with others who are committed to the same goals. When we look either at the past or at our own limitations, we can easily lose sight of what God is up to. As we see with the selection process for David, God often focuses on what's inside us, who we are and the way we're made, rather than what's outside us, our circumstances or weaknesses.

God chooses each of us from the inside out just as he chose David. God is not limited by our regrets, by our lack of confidence, by our confusion, or by our uncertainty. He has placed seeds of greatness in each person he's created; he's made us in his image to accomplish amazing feats. Each of us has a vision; some of us are dreaming dreams. All of us have the ability to turn away, but God's purpose will provide a clear pathway to a better future.

And, as Peter, Samuel, and David illustrate for us, God uses ordinary people—with all their flaws and problems—to accomplish extraordinary dreams. You and I don't have to wait until we have it all together, achieve a certain degree of fame, earn a specified amount of money, get a better job, or meet the right person. Instead, we can start today to embrace who we are and how God made us, knowing that he will use us. From this knowledge, wellsprings of confidence water our hearts. That confidence allows us to see our dreams and visions as God's road maps to significant lives. And at the very moment we recognize and acknowledge his plans in our present, we begin to establish an eternal foundation for our confidence.

So, in order to start living a more significant life, assess where you are right now, where you want to be, and the confidence you need to get there. Real change is possible in our lives if we're willing to move beyond our past mistakes and work through any present disappointments. We must also let go of our own limited expectations about the way God works in our lives and allow ourselves to be surprised by him. After all, if we're focused on his presence in our lives and intent on pursuing our relationships with him in the midst of community, then who we were meant to be will emerge more clearly every day. *It's never too late to change and begin experiencing the fullness of a life filled with joy and peace, a life built on the bedrock of confidence in God.*

# CHAPTER 2

# The Confidence to Grow

When we're clearly moving in the direction of God's will, we receive inspiration to move confidently forward in his significant plans for us. However, our responses during times of uncertainty and doubt, times when we haven't a clue about what God is up to or when he doesn't seem to be answering our prayers, may tell us more about our actual level of confidence in him.

During such hard times we can find ourselves questioning our value, wondering, "Is my life *really* significant? Do I really matter to him? How can I keep trusting him when life is so hard?" When these questions arise in my own mind or I hear about other people wrestling with their faith, my friends Eric and Pam Cuellar come to mind.

A couple of years ago, Pam was coming to the end of a full-term pregnancy and had every reason to expect a normal labor. After fifteen minutes in the hospital waiting room, though, Eric was stunned to see Pam being rushed into surgery. The nurse followed and informed the father-to-be that his wife required an emergency C-section.

Eric immediately began to pray—and of course he desperately wanted to see Pam and his new son. A few minutes later, a doctor came out and told Eric that Pam was fine, but that the baby had no vital signs. Things didn't look good, the doctor said, but they were working on resuscitating the baby. Upon hearing this news, Eric immediately began pleading with God to bring life to his baby boy, and Eric knew that in the next room Pam was crying out the same request.

Generally, doctors spend about fifteen minutes trying to bring life to a stillborn, and the staff worked diligently on that child for those nine hundred seconds, but to no avail: the baby was not breathing. In the sixteenth minute, though, the baby's eyes dilated. *Maybe there's a slight chance,* the doctor thought. Two hours later, there was still a spark of life in little Zander, so the doctor ordered him airlifted to a hospital better suited to his needs.

By the time Eric and Pam arrived at the other hospital, the diagnosis was grim. Their little boy—with wires and tubes enveloping every part of his small body—was medically paralyzed. "Don't hope for very much," the doctor said. "Your child is very sick." Eric and Pam thanked the doctor but went on to say that they had been praying and that they believed nothing was impossible for God. And, as their very sick baby lay in the hospital, the Cuellars kept praying.

One day went by, and nothing changed. Two days, and still no improvement. For nine days there was little or no change in Zander Cuellar's condition. By this time, however, his parents weren't the only ones praying. Our church as well as others across Texas were lifting this family up. But that baby boy just continued to rest there, tubes zigzagging over and around his tiny body, showing little, if any, reason for hope.

Let me stop for a moment and ask you to consider what you'd be feeling if you were in Pam and Eric's shoes. Where are most of us after nine days of prayer? How strong is our trust in God when he seems silent? Do we have any hope left at all? Do we opt for skepticism and forsake the hope we have in him? Hope can be such a dangerous thing because of how vulnerable it makes us. Proverbs 13:12 tells us, "Hope deferred makes the heart sick." Perhaps hope is so difficult to manage because inherent in it is a measure of expectation that we can't deny. Like the Cuellars, we want to expect the best even when the evidence around us doesn't support our hope. We're often afraid to hope, as I suspect Pam and Eric were when they faced the possibility of such a heartbreaking loss. And as it is with prayer, things often don't make sense to us, limited as we are by our human perspective.

But the Cuellars wouldn't give up the fight, wouldn't let go of their faith, wouldn't deny that the miraculous could still happen. And let me tell you, when that baby took his first breath on the tenth day, that breath let loose praise across southeast Texas that must have been music to God's ears! So many of us had prayed despite our fears and discouragement, and when Zander took his first breath, no one asked whether the investment in prayer was worth it. Every single one of us danced for joy! God had answered our prayers; we knew he had done the seemingly impossible. When the medical reports and test results came back, we learned that, in response to those prayers, our powerful God had healed collapsed lungs, a defective heart valve, excess fluid, septic infection, and a depressed immune system.

Does the initial diagnosis prevail now? No! God moved and definitively spoke his will into Zander Cuellar's life. And every person who prayed for that child knows God created confidence in those who took part. Experiences such as this one with Zander, his family, and our community illustrate how confidence moves us from the creation stage to the building stage.

## UNDER CONSTRUCTION

This construction process—this building up of our confidence in God—occurs in each of us as God demonstrates his faithfulness and ongoing direction for our lives even as we experience painful and disappointing events. God wants to grow our confidence into maturity and stretch our faith so that it becomes stronger. He wants us to give him our hope and trust so that he can show us his power and goodness. With each provision and miracle, our confidence becomes stronger and more adaptable to the hard things ahead.

Of course not every infant born with challenges survives, and I'm certainly not implying that not getting the miracle we were praying and hoping for means we lacked faith or didn't pray fervently enough. Nor am I implying that God wants us to suffer as a means of testing us or while he decides who he's going to help. Our God is a loving God, and even when we can't imagine how he could allow a baby to die or a tsunami to devastate an entire nation, we must acknowledge that we don't know everything about everything. He is the sovereign God, and we are his creation, not the other way around.

Especially when the miracle doesn't happen the way we hoped and prayed it would and we experience loss and pain, we must not let those times obstruct our view of God and his ability to work in our lives. If we're willing to trust God, even with our greatest losses, he can use personal tragedies to build our faith and create deeper confidence in his character and sovereignty.

Seeing the way God released his faithfulness to us in past trials builds the confidence we need now when we don't see answers—when the baby lies listlessly between life and death, when our marriages seem to be on emotional life support, or when the plug gets pulled on our job. Each time we experience God's provision, his timing, or his sovereignty, the infrastructure of our faith grows. Such faith is like a mighty tower that enables us to rise above our limited human perspective. We are elevated as we remember and honor occasions in the past when the Lord blessed us, answered our prayers, or revealed his plan for us.

## ENTRY-LEVEL CONFIDENCE

Certainly one of the gifts to us in God's Word is the ability to see God's goodness and sovereignty spread out over so many centuries of human history. We witness this, for instance, as we return to David, one of my favorite examples of a person who lived a significant life. In him we see a confidence cultivated by his ability to trust God in the gaps. The main reason David went from being a poor shepherd to Israel's most beloved king was his ability to recognize his calling and handle it with care. David's tower of faith grew with each lion and bear he killed to protect his sheep, with each Goliath he defeated, with each time he ducked another javelin thrown at him by Saul. David had plenty of opportunities to bail out, but he chose to stay the course because he—like the Cuellars—knew the hope of a plan bigger than his own.

David's confidence came from knowing and accepting the dream God had for him, not just from his own dreams or others' dreams for him. Not only does God assign each one of us a purpose, but he also creates the path for us to follow in order to fulfill that purpose.

As we'll see time and time again in the life of David, God longs for us to discover our true callings and to live eternally significant lives. But God doesn't just show us our purposes without giving us clues about how to proceed. Instead, he prepares us for and then provides for us each step of the way. That's why *we can experience significant lives throughout our journeys, not just from reaching one particular destination.* With this in mind, look at one of the first classrooms that God used to prepare David for his destiny:

> Now the Spirit of the LORD had departed from Saul, and an evil spirit from the LORD tormented him.
>
> Saul's attendants said to him, "See, an evil spirit from God is tormenting you. Let our lord command his servants here to search for someone who can play the harp. He will play when the evil spirit from God comes upon you, and you will feel better."
>
> So Saul said to his attendants, "Find someone who plays well and bring him to me." (1 Samuel 16:14–16)

God had called David to be king, but David began his journey to the throne with an entry-level position. Imagine for a moment how you'd respond if Samuel had anointed your head with oil and said, "God has chosen you to be king over his people." Some of us might be tempted to say, "All right! Let's get on with this king business! I was made for the royal life!" Others of us might be more interested in proving ourselves: "I'm ready to go! I'll show everyone that I'm going to be the best king ever." Still others of us, those more toward the humble end of the spectrum, might be so overwhelmed by the prospect of ruling Israel that we're speechless. The important point here, though, is to realize that our calling first presents itself as an opportunity. With this approach, God makes sure the calling is received as our responsibility and not merely as our privilege, as our partnership with him and not just as a solo performance.

David started being king when he began serving King Saul. Who better to become a leader than someone who has first learned to be a follower? That's why confidence must start at the entry level. We've all had entry-level positions, both personally and professionally, and they usually feel beneath us: *I'm not washing those dishes, I'm not changing diapers, I'm not flipping burgers every day for the rest of my life.* But how we treat our entry-level responsibilities determines how we will handle problems as fathers, mothers, bosses, CEOs, or kings. And when we approach with confidence the entry-level times of our lives, our humility and obedience often expand our visions so that God can use us to open doors of opportunity in bigger ways. If we're willing to serve at the entry level, then God promotes us beyond our wildest imaginations. Put differently, we are noticed for doing our initial tasks well, and then we are entrusted with more responsibility.

## RECOGNIZED FOR WHO WE ARE

Even though he was chosen by God for what was in his heart, David still faced some barriers on his way to the throne. He wasn't born into a royal family where he would have simply and indisputably inherited the position. As we've seen, David's situation was just the opposite; he came from a humble family of shepherds. So it took time for the people of Israel to recognize David and his many abilities, including giftedness, positive attitude, and faithfulness. When others see that we're moving in accordance with our God-given purposes, they become aware of opportunities where we're needed. Interestingly enough, God uses these opportunities as stepping stones for where he is leading us and the larger goals he wants us to accomplish. Here's how David began taking some of those first steps:

> One of the servants answered, "I have seen a son of Jesse of Bethlehem who knows how to play the harp. He is a brave man and a warrior. He speaks well and is a fine-looking man. And the LORD is with him." (1 Samuel 16:18)

Upon this servant's recommendation, Saul sends messengers to Jesse's household to retrieve the boy. These men saw David as the world saw him: a brave, good-looking warrior and talented musician. With Saul as his boss, though, the servant who spoke up about David probably would have kept quiet had he known God's plans for the shepherd boy. Unaware, this servant played a key role in elevating this young shepherd to a place where he would be a king in training—utilizing and reinforcing the gifts and calling that God gave him.

This incident in David's life reminds me of a friend of mine who's responsible for the hiring at a large corporation. He has hiring down to a formula: if you have a high school diploma, then he wants you to have at least three months work experience before he'll interview you. If you have a college degree, then you need to have been out in the work force at least nine months before he'll consider you for his company. If you have a graduate degree, then he wants to see on your résumé at least a year in the field.

His explanation intrigues me. "The degree isn't enough to impress me," he says. "I want to see a commitment to excellence, and that's only displayed after the degree has been earned." This perspective seemed strange to me at first because we usually think that having a college or graduate degree entitles us to a higher position. But my friend insists that what people do after receiving their degrees is what indicates their potential value to his company.

Even if you don't agree with my friend's hiring system, you can't argue his point that excellence demands commitment. And excellence gets noticed as our talents are transformed into skills. A person may have a talent for hitting a baseball, but skilled players hit a baseball consistently at every level they play. They hit it because they have worked at it. Quite often, all that talented people like David need is an opportunity to become skilled. Once they seize that opportunity, their faithful efforts to develop their talents lead to greater confidence.

## GROWTH FORMULA

God made David a warrior, God made him a musician, and God made him handsome. God also put a call on his life, and when that call came, David continually moved forward because he met with courage the opportunities God put in his path. Notice, for instance, how David progressed in his dealings with King Saul:

> Saul liked him very much, and David became one of his
> armor-bearers. Then Saul sent word to Jesse, saying, "Allow
> David to remain in my service, for I am pleased with him."

> Whenever the spirit from God came upon Saul, David
> would take his harp and play. Then relief would come to
> Saul; he would feel better, and the evil spirit would leave him.
> (1 Samuel 16:21–23)

As he served in the court of King Saul, David set aside any potential feelings of entitlement or inferiority, the two extremes that tend to close in on us as we advance. Instead, he courageously and humbly moved into the opportunities presented to him. David apparently regarded each day as an opportunity to trust God and live significantly. Similarly, my friends the Cuellars regarded a potential crisis in their lives as this same kind of opportunity. Their faith in God sustained them through a time of uncertainty and fear, and their son is living and breathing today because of it. Life had not given Eric and Pam what they expected—just as David's initial position with Saul was not exactly what he planned. But, given the chance to couple their perseverence with their faith in God, the Cuellars moved into the crisis courageously and transformed the life of their child as well as the lives of the people around them.

The responses of David and people like the Cuellars serve as powerful models for the rest of us. Like me, you've probably seen numerous examples where people are only confident when their performances bring immediate results. When situations aren't quickly resolved, these people often fall apart. Soon they become afraid that their worlds can't be different, so they back away from new opportunities that come their way and bury their talents inside. I've learned that instead of letting our fears and uncertainties immobilize us, we should praise God for the way our situations can bring us new opportunities to trust him more fully and to grow in our confidence.

In fact, I've developed a little formula that captures this process of growing in confidence and creating forward momentum as we pursue our dreams. The formula has helped me relate to my four children in a way that nurtures confidence and releases their potential.

First, potential watered by encouragement grows and blooms into purposeful passion. The passion to work is then natural and not forced. Second, as our "passion fruit" becomes focused on God's goals, we develop the priorities necessary to accomplish those objectives. This process then continues as we grow stronger and more confident in God's character as well as in who he's created us to be. The formula looks something like this:

$$(\textbf{Praise} + \textbf{Potential}) \times (\textbf{Passion} + \textbf{Priorities}) = \textbf{Progress}$$

Of course mapping these concepts out is easier than living them out, but I hope this equation helps. (And please excuse all the *p*'s, but you know how pastors love alliteration!) The goal is to see that living significant lives requires the development of our potential. And in order to blossom, that potential needs praise, the kind of positive reinforcement that God usually provides through others. As our potential—recognized and reinforced by others—matures, we develop passion for who we are and what God calls us to accomplish. This passion fuels our recognition of certain choices we must make if we are to fulfill our goals; put simply, this passion determines our priorities, our choices about how we spend our time and other resources. I think that's why God doesn't ask us to be successful; rather he asks us to be obedient to his purposes, knowing that will produce the success he created us to experience.

So how does our confidence become a steady source of motivation for living significant lives? I believe that when we recognize a trial, problem, or hardship as an opportunity to exercise our faith in God, we begin to allow him to manifest his greatness. As we learn to release ourselves from what is humanly possible and instead dare to hope for that which seems impossible, this confidence in God's love and power allows him to construct something beautiful in our lives.

Hold on to this truth now as you consider those areas of life where you're presently struggling. What is keeping you from trusting God? What can you do to continue to exercise your faith in him even though you can't tell what he's up to? I believe the key lies in choosing to believe that he's accomplishing a greater purpose than you can imagine. Perhaps the conflicts at your job are preparing you for a promotion. Maybe the argument with your spouse can improve communication and strengthen your marriage. Please don't hear these words as simplistic, Pollyanna-type encouragement to look for the silver lining in every cloud.

Instead, remember two truths: *our perspective is limited, but our God is unlimited.* We can only see part of the picture—one frame of the movie—at a time, but God sees it all. And although our resources may be limited, our faith stretched, and our fears multiplied, our Father can provide for all our needs, and he delights in loving us more than we can know. He is the ultimate chief of the construction crew of our lives, and he builds and shapes, tears down whatever is unneeded or in the way, and constructs a masterpiece, a work of significance, out of our lives. Under his direction, we can have the confidence to grow into all that we were meant to be.

# CHAPTER 3

# The Confidence to Endure

I once got to sit down with some of Hollywood's most successful film producers—real heavy hitters, multimillionaires at the top of their game. I took the opportunity to ask them about their beginnings and discovered that they, like David, started very young, just by living out their passion in the backyard. They took their families' video camera, built sets, and made movies about everything they could find: brothers, sisters, rocks, trees, imaginary battles between Barbie and G.I. Joe, and all sorts of neighborhood mysteries. Regardless of the kinds of films they enjoyed making or the number of successful films they had completed, those successful producers acknowledged that their visions started with potential and passion, and then they started climbing.

Professionally, almost every single one of those particular executives started in the industry at the entry level: holding lights, running errands, tearing down sets. My producer friend said, for instance, "I made commercials, and somebody saw them. When they called me for an interview, I took everything I had ever done along with me, and I dropped it in their laps." His interviewers later said they hired my friend because he didn't talk about what he could do; rather, he demonstrated what he had done!

The combination of our visions, our dreams, and our potential results in confidence when we take the risk and act. This combination also provides a foundation for growing our talents into skills. After all, how many people talk about what they are going to do, but never do it? They want to start a business or create a new ministry. They talk about the husband or wife they wish they could be but overlook the small daily details of service and respect. Similarly, many of us plan on doing better by our kids—we want to attend more ball games, spend more time at home, discuss important matters with them—but then become too busy to do much more than kiss them goodnight. Good intentions aren't enough. That's why we have a motto at my house: "Don't talk about the good family you want to have someday. Instead, become a better family member today." *Confidence grows naturally when where we are growing in our competence.*

## ENGINE MAINTENANCE

As we experience God building confidence into our lives, we need to remember that our confidence shouldn't stop growing simply because we've achieved some measure of success. Just because we've built the engine and can drive the car doesn't mean we don't have to continue filling the tank with gas, checking the oil level, and making sure the belts and filters are in good shape. Whether mechanically inclined or not, we all know that you have to maintain an engine to keep it running smoothly.

Confidence is the same way. We have to maintain our confidence level in order for it to help us get where we want to go. Consider now the engine of David's life. He went from being a lowly shepherd boy, whose potential was overlooked by his father and brothers, to being a harpist to the king, to being the king's messenger boy, to being a warrior, and ultimately to being king. It's an underdog story, the kind of heroic epic that movie executives can make millions from by creating it on the big screen. Who wouldn't like to go from rags to riches? David's the Cinderella, rags-to-riches story we all know and love.

But with any success story, ugly details sometimes get lost in the glorious shuffle. Even when someone becomes successful, that person's story is hardly over. (Where would movie executives be without movie sequels?) In the life of David specifically, those details are important because they show us how to maintain confidence so we can draw on it when we need it. Now we know that God exalted David because he wanted to bless Israel with a godly king. But we often overlook the fact that David had many opportunities to fall short, and he sometimes did. But he consistently demonstrated an ongoing commitment to confident living in the midst of life's pressures. In fact, David's life illustrates that maintaining our confidence is necessary and vital to how we grow and serve.

David clearly exemplifies that facing battles bigger than ourselves is one of the fruits of confidence's courage. In other words, these trials solidify our confidence in our lives. David started with a reputation for being God's chosen one, a fierce warrior, and poetic musician. But he couldn't rest on his laurels and just coast through the rest of his life. No matter how much our confidence has grown from past victories, we need strategies for maintaining our confidence when life throws new obstacles our way.

## DISARMING DISCONTENT

And new obstacles come in various sizes. How, for instance, do you respond when you are in bumper-to-bumper traffic going no miles an hour? when your flight is delayed and you're stuck in an uncomfortable chair in the airport? when your doctor is running late and keeps you fuming in the waiting room for over an hour? Most of us grow very impatient and have a tough time getting beyond our discontent about the situation. We often feel powerless and don't know what to do, and that frustration increases our discontent as we wait.

I'm confident that David understood what it means to wait and to wonder when it will be time to move on. As we've seen, after Samuel anointed David as future king, this shepherd boy went to work for Saul. Interestingly enough, though, in between working for Saul and becoming king, David still had to work the family farm:

> Jesse had eight sons…, [and the] three oldest sons had followed Saul to the war [against the Philistines],…but David went back and forth from Saul to tend his father's sheep in Bethlehem. (1 Samuel 17:12–15)

Talk about a downer! David knew he was destined to become king, but he found himself having to pick up after his daddy's sheep. This isn't rags to riches; this is rags to better rags and then back to scrubbing toilets with those rags! Most of us don't deal well with going backward. Once we've placed a foot on the next rung of the ladder, it's tough to go back down a step or two. Yet Scripture doesn't record anything about David responding negatively in this situation. Instead it shows him doing what he needs to despite any moments of discontent.

This ability to face our present boredom is something we must all learn to practice. Unexpected situations, though, are only one cause of discontent. Consider a time when you wanted something badly and worked hard to get it. Maybe you wanted a new home or a better job. Maybe you wanted to be out of debt or back in school. But then once you achieved your goal, you felt a letdown in your spirit as you realized that your life wasn't as improved as you'd thought it would be.

Such is the nature of discontent, and I believe that discontent is a key contributor to our feeling insignificant. We can joke about the cliché of the grass always being greener on the other side. Yet the promise of the greener grass bombards us daily. Don't like the way you look? Then buy this jacket or try this hair color. Don't like the way others perceive you? Then buy this SUV or live in this gated neighborhood. Many businesses, particularly in the advertising and entertainment industries, count on the fact that we human beings tend to always be on the lookout for the next big thing we want; these industries capitalize on their awareness that we are never fully content with how life is going.

Bottom line, like termites eroding the tower that you've worked so hard to build, discontent can destroy our confidence. The structure may look sound from the outside, but we know that, inside, we're not satisfied. Discontent can also carry with it fear and uncertainty that will ravage our sense of personal significance and our awareness of who we truly are. We see this happen when David approached the Israelite forces who were shaking in their boots because of Goliath:

> Goliath, the Philistine champion from Gath, stepped out
> from his lines and shouted his usual defiance, and David
> heard it. When the Israelites saw the man, they all ran from
> him in great fear. (1 Samuel 17:23–24)

The Israelites had no confidence in God or in themselves as they stood before the threatening Philistine giant. There they were, veteran warriors facing a problem they had been trained to solve. Have you ever been there? "Wait a second," you say in the face of a problem at work. "We've solved problems before, but today I'm overwhelmed and I just want to quit." Situations we could beat—situations at work, in our families, in our friendships, in our churches—subtly intimidate us and deflate our confidence. Like the Israelites, we often stand there scratching our heads and feeling too intimidated to take action. But as he looked at Goliath, David said, "Wait a second! Who does this bully think he is? He's not of God, so what are we afraid of?" David didn't let discontent steal his desire to be daring.

"Let's go, fight, win" is the attitude of someone living a significant life, and that was the attitude David exemplified on the battlefield. Significant people, particularly when serving in a leadership role, must remind those around them of the dreams God has called them to pursue. Those leaders must turn others' attention back to something larger than the obstacles now standing in their way. That's why, in this scene with David, it's not surprising to see him call the Israelites back to reality. For you see, the reality of how God works, not the fantasy of our fears and flaws, is the real battleground of faith. And often the battles aren't due to outside threats but emerge from within our own communities. The minute David spoke up, his critics—chicken-hearted as they were—criticized him:

> When Eliab, David's oldest brother, heard him speaking with
> the men, he burned with anger at him and asked, "Why have
> you come down here? And with whom did you leave those
> few sheep in the desert? I know how conceited you are and
> how wicked your heart is; you came down only to watch the
> battle." (1 Samuel 17:28)

Forget the fact that David was bringing the guy lunch! But know that according to ancient Jewish tradition, Eliab should have been the one anointed king. It was his right as the firstborn son. So, naturally, Eliab was ticked. David, his little brother, had already outshone him by being chosen by God, and there was nothing Eliab could do about it.

Remember when Jesse had to call David from the fields for Samuel to anoint him? Jesse hadn't even considered David as a serious contender for God's fullest blessing. And now David's older brother was telling him to mind his own business. Not many people can sustain such rejection and still move forward in a productive way. But living out our significance requires embracing our full potential even when it isn't esteemed by others.

## Deactivating Discouragement

David had the choice to cut and run or stay and fight. From the tone of the passage, it appears he can't fathom but one option—to come out swinging and fight for what he believes. Even in the midst of peer pressure and criticism from his big brother, David went to Saul and said, "Somebody has to fight!" And the king, like all the rest of David's audience, basically said, "You're just a kid, David. You couldn't possibly know what you're talking about." This patronizing response—intended no doubt to remind David that he was too naive to know what was feasible in the real world—would have discouraged many people.

In fact, plenty of people would have stopped trying to deal with their Goliaths—for reasons they felt were quite legitimate: "My family never believed in me," "My job didn't work out the way it was supposed to", "My boss is a jerk," "My friends told me I couldn't do it." Everybody knows rejection, and many of us use our experiences with rejection as reasons to quit. But Scripture reminds us to guard our hearts (see Proverbs 4:23). If we don't, discouragement erases courage from our hearts. We do it to ourselves—other people don't discourage us. My father taught me to remember that if my courage was ever stolen, it was always an inside job.

So David approached his challenge as people of courage do: he knew he was obligated to act according to the dream God had given him. Hear what this young shepherd boy said to King Saul:

> Let no one lose heart on account of this Philistine; your servant will go and fight him.... Your servant has killed both the lion and the bear [while tending sheep]; this uncircumcised Philistine will be like one of them, because he has defied the armies of the living God. The LORD who delivered me from the paw of a lion and the paw of the bear will deliver me from the hand of this Philistine. (1 Samuel 17:32, 36–37)

David truly was a humble servant, and his humility was clearly key to his confidence. He did what servants are called of God to do: he served his master well. Many of us think our masters are here on this earth—just as David's boss, King Saul, was—but David's confidence was rooted in his understanding that God's will included his earthly master's business. God knew better than Saul or anyone else what David needed to do. So David's confidence, bred in his humble beginnings as a shepherd, was emboldened by his humble submission to God's plans. He was willing to yield to what the Lord asked of him, even in the face of unlikely, if not impossible, odds.

In many instances we—like David—must make the choice to be confident. That choice requires courage, and that courage requires seasoning, and that seasoning requires preparation. David knew and trusted that God prepares those whom he calls to carry out his great works, and David realized that his past experience had prepared him for the exact task at hand. David had battled wild animals to their death—no small accomplishment in itself—but he apparently never said, "I've had it with this shepherding business." He constantly battled, persevering and waiting, trusting that some future conflict would require the skills he was honing. As he faced Goliath, David's courage and preparation in the past moved him forward when others feared and failed. David chose to deactivate the discouragement he had many reasons to feel.

## Deflating Depression

Like discouragement, depression can also sap our confidence. Being told to stay positive, to keep a stiff upper lip, or to look at the bright side can sound like such empty platitudes. Besides, we all experience seasons in life when we grieve a loss or encounter a disappointment, and sadness is appropriate. We must, however, be on guard for the subtle ways that depression can undermine our confidence in ourselves, in God, and in those we love.

We certainly learn from the different ways Saul and David dealt with depression. Basically, Saul didn't overcome his sorrow. He had lost his vision and didn't try to recapture it through fellowship with the Lord or godly people. Consequently Saul found himself vulnerable, the Spirit of the Lord departed, and soon Saul and his soldiers lived sapped of courage.

When Goliath stood there once again taunting his troops, Saul was in his tent. David wondered, *What's in this for the guy who beats this monster?* And the quivering soldiers stood there knowing what it would take to get Saul's dignity back:

The king will give great wealth to the man who kills
[Goliath]. He will also give him his daughter in marriage
and will exempt his father's family from taxes in Israel.
(1 Samuel 17:25)

David certainly didn't need this extra incentive to enter this fight. He
knew it was what God wanted him to do. He also knew something about
what it takes to get others invested as well as to allow them to save face.

The soldiers of Israel, however, lacked confidence because they couldn't
see beyond their own abilities to grasp God's purpose. The soldiers' lack of
confidence in themselves was based on their own experiences; they didn't
possess the firm foundation of supernatural confidence. Living under the
cloud of Saul's depression as well as giving in to their own fear and uncertainty, these men could only stand there and come up with reasons to back
away.

David, on the other hand, stood his ground and jumped right in. We
see here the difference between someone who says, "Maybe we should try…
No, that won't work," and someone who says, "Let's just do it! Let's make
something great happen right now!" David had developed and matured his
confidence, so he was ready to act on it. David knew that God's will superseded other people's opinions and that God was intent on proving it.

Saul—like Jesse, Eliab, and probably David's other six brothers—allowed
their confidence to be shaped by the world's perceptions and standards.
They also permitted unhealthy human relationships to cloud God's will.
They had every reason to believe that God would empower them, but they
didn't choose to exercise faith and listen to his voice.

It's worth noting here that David didn't try to battle their negativity.
Instead he fought the giant that caused the pessimism. David didn't even

accept Saul's offer of the royal armor and sword when he faced the terrible giant. Instead David chose the weapon with which he was familiar—the slingshot that he had used on the hillsides to protect his sheep. When we face a crisis, using equipment other than what God has given us may be tempting. We must, however, remember that God is the One who equips us and that he provides all we need to face any problem.

David knew this truth. He was living a significant life in pursuit of God's dream, and he couldn't let discontent, discouragement, and depression infect the nation of Israel and destroy it from within. So David did for Israel what Samuel did for him: he gave them a vision for what they could become. David's story reminds us that giants will loom over us at key moments throughout our lives. We must never lose sight of our ability—through God's power—to pick up a slingshot and fight.

> As the Philistine moved closer to attack him, David ran
> quickly toward the battle line to meet him. Reaching into
> his bag and taking out a stone, he slung it and struck the
> Philistine on the forehead. The stone sank into his forehead,
> and he fell facedown on the ground.
>
> So David triumphed over the Philistine with a sling and a
> stone; without a sword in his hand he struck down the Philis-
> tine and killed him. (1 Samuel 17:48–50)

David maintained his confidence by demonstrating it each day. That's why he was able to draw upon his reserves of confidence, courage, and resourcefulness and why he knew he could overcome even the most intimidating enemy. But for too many people the drive to fight is gone before the battle even begins. They want a better tomorrow, but they wait for God to move in some overt and dramatic way. While God sometimes does accomplish his goals that way, more often he uses his people to accomplish them—as we act on our passions and exercise our gifts each day. In Psalm 37, David wrote, "Delight yourself in the LORD and he will give you the desires of your heart" (verse 4). If we delight in the Lord even when we're discouraged or overwhelmed, he sustains us.

## DEEP ROOTS

We can learn much about confidence from David. Instead of selling himself into the slavery of others' opinions, for instance, David showed those around him what it meant to live a life of significance. He wasn't arrogant or conceited, but he also didn't waste time and energy battling against people or in his own power. Instead he set his heart on God's dream, Samuel's vision, and his potential.

David also drew on two powerful complementary power sources in overcoming a seemingly impossible opponent: confidence rooted in his past experiences and confidence from his Creator. David knew—and acted boldly in the knowledge—that God prepares us so that we can face and overcome the challenges of life. In order to live significant lives, we must therefore keep our eyes fixed on him and move confidently out into the world around us.

As we conclude this chapter and this section on confidence, I encourage you to examine the ways you see yourself and see God working in your life. Are you part of a godly community of contagious dreamers? (We'll look more closely at the importance of community in our final section, but I hope people around you share your dreams and partner with you in serving God to accomplish them.) Have you embraced the vision for your life that God has set before you? Do you trust his faithfulness enough to continue building your confidence in him as well as in who he created and has called you to be? What will you do to battle the deadly Ds of discontent, discouragement, and depression and thereby preserve your confidence? What do you see as the ultimate source of the confidence necessary to live a significant life—and what will you do to draw upon that source as you fight your daily battles?

I am confident that God has called you—and has promised to strengthen you—to do this work. So don't waste any more days. *God will do something special with your life if you will exercise faith in living out your purpose.* If you discover how he's gifted you and where he's calling you, and if you glimpse what he's up to, your confidence will grow with deep roots, roots that will see you through the droughts of doubt and the winters of wondering why you're here on this earth. Move boldly into your future, my friend, infused with the confidence that the Creator of the universe made you unlike anyone else for a special purpose that is yours alone!

# PART II

## Character

LORD, who may dwell in your sanctuary?
Who may live on your holy hill?

He whose walk is blameless
and who does what is righteous,
who speaks the truth from his heart
and has no slander on his tongue,
who does his neighbor no wrong
and casts no slur on his fellowman,
who despises a vile man
but honors those who fear the LORD,
who keeps his oath
even when it hurts,
who lends his money without usury
and does not accept a bribe against the innocent.

He who does these things
will never be shaken.

PSALM 15

# CHAPTER 4

## Behave in the Cave

Like many people, I enjoy reading history and getting glimpses into the famous moments and world events that have significantly impacted how we live today. I'm often amazed by how one individual's decision, belief, or conviction can be the catalyst for profound change. The tipping point in a life often seems to depend on an individual leader's character—not just what he or she believes, but what the person is made of in the core of his or her being. Noble dreams often spark transforming movements when the leader faces circumstances that require great sacrifice.

For instance, most of us recognize Abraham Lincoln's incredible leadership during the Civil War (or the War Between the States, as my American history professor insisted on calling it). Lincoln was surely one of those rare individuals who could maintain the course during even the darkest moments. But if you read any number of his biographies, you'll see that Mr. Lincoln *suffered*—I mean roiled and ached with emotional and physical pain—during the four long years our country warred against itself.

Think about what those years must have been like! Imagine believing in something so passionately that you stand your ground even as friends and loved ones criticize you and others die fighting for your cause. This kind of suffering would exhaust anyone, and Lincoln did suffer from severe depression. That depression was fueled in part by personal tragedies, especially the death of his twelve-year-old son, Willie, in 1862, right in the middle of the war. To be able to lead the country in its darkest hour—despite such grief and anguish—requires a fortitude and stamina not often reported in our instant sound-bite culture. Four years is a long time to fight for what you know to be true, especially when the cost for that belief is being paid in human lives. But President Lincoln stood strong, and our country thrives today because of who he was.

## No Small Parts

You may be thinking to yourself, "Jim, I'm no Abraham Lincoln. I'm just trying to earn a living for my family and serve God in my community. I don't have that kind of strength of character. Besides, isn't character something heroes need?"

Yes, character is something heroes need, but not just larger-than-life heroes: heroes like you and me who keep putting one foot in front of the other as we earn our livings and serve our Lord in the everyday world. That's why God develops character in us throughout our lifetime. So wherever you are today, recognize God is trying to cultivate in you the character necessary to fulfill your God-given purpose. And that truth isn't obvious to everyone, so think with me a moment about an observation a friend recently made. He spoke of how, as modern warfare developed, men tried to build bigger and bigger bombs. But some scientists began to suggest that the greatest power was in the smallest place—in the atom. Sure enough, when scientists figured out how to release the potential inherent in atoms, staggering never-before-seen power was unleashed.

Character is that way. Study its effect on individual lives, families, and even nations, and you will stand in awe of its power. Just as Lincoln's character was a vital contributor to the *United* States we live in today, your character is a vital contributor to the significant life you are yearning to lead. Character is what God needs in us as we strive toward significance, and it will be tested because the world is filled with jealous, compromising, scheming people.

In David's case, one character test came as a civil war was fought. Saul, the king whose own son "became one in spirit with David" (1 Samuel 18:1), quickly viewed David as a threat. David's success caused his reputation to exceed Saul's, and Saul's insecurity got the best of him:

> Saul was afraid of David, because the LORD was with David
> but had left Saul. So he sent David away from him and gave
> him command over a thousand men, and David led the
> troops in their campaigns. In everything he did he had great
> success, because the LORD was with him. When Saul saw how
> successful he was, he was afraid of him. But all Israel and
> Judah loved David, because he led them in their campaigns.
> (1 Samuel 18:12–16)

To eliminate the problem, Saul offered David his daughter in marriage, but the bridal price he set required a battle in which Saul hoped David would die. When David survived, Saul got a little more direct: he threw a spear at David while he was playing the harp (see 19:9). Unsuccessful, Saul then sent troops to his son-in-law's house in an attempt to kill him. Yet David never struck back at Saul.

These kinds of dramatic obstacles may not apply to all of us as we grapple with becoming people of significance. But you see, *people of character do right regardless* of how large or small the obstacles are. D. L. Moody once stated, "Character is what you do in the dark." He knew that real character is only proven as we remain true in the midst of trials and temptations *when no one is looking.*

Knowing that Saul was God's man for the job at the moment, David remained true to King Saul despite the threats and attempts on his life. When David was finally forced to flee for his life, he ran to people who reinforced his convictions, not his cynicism. He sought help from Samuel, the man who had anointed him a few years earlier, and later from the godly priest Ahimelech. *What passion and potential are to confidence, right people and right purposes are to character.* Even so, David—the man of godly character—found himself alone in a cave.

## CAVE CHARACTER

As I mentioned earlier, I spent the early years of my ministry preaching throughout Africa and Europe. My first trip was a ten-week visit to Uganda, a big culture shock for one who had never before been out of the United States. Uganda was in the midst of a civil war, and I'm sure many of you have heard something about the Idi Amin massacres. Numerous articles describing his brutal reign have been written, and a movie was produced depicting some of the atrocities.

By the time I arrived in Uganda, Idi Amin had fled the country. However, the nation was still fighting a civil war, and evidence of the pain and suffering he'd brought to people's lives could be seen everywhere. Bullet holes in churches reminded Christians of the believers Amin had tortured in prison camps, and nearly everyone spoke of someone they loved who had been killed in the fighting. Soldiers were still looting people's homes and murdering innocent civilians.

One night I heard the screams of an innocent victim in my neighborhood. When I arose in the morning, I learned that his family was planning his funeral. My first thought was, *Lord, should I go back to graduate school?* I knew my family thought I was crazy to go to Uganda in the first place, and now I was definitely ready to leave.

I'm so glad I didn't leave, though, before I met a man who is a hero to me. Jotham Mutebi, like David, is a man whose life shows the power inherent in character. Besides pastoring a church in Masaka, Uganda, he was vice president of a large church-planting operation in Uganda and therefore a target of Idi Amin's religious aggression. His congregation watched as Pastor Mutebi was dragged off to a prison camp where most of the inhabitants died.

Pastor Mutebi told me many things I will never tell anyone, things he had told nobody else but felt compelled to share with me since I willingly lived in danger in his country. I agree with him that people don't need to know all the brutal details, but I will say that the atrocities he described were almost unbelievable. That human beings can treat each other as horribly as he described is a terrible reality.

Part of Pastor Mutebi's story, though, will help us discover the power character has in living significant lives. While the pastor was in prison camp, a guard demanded that he smoke a cigarette. The act might seem like a small thing to many people, but it was a big deal to Pastor Mutebi.

Believing that God was calling him to stand up to the darkness, he refused to smoke. The prison guard threatened to shoot him if he didn't smoke, and all the prisoners knew that the guard might do just that. They encouraged Pastor Mutebi to smoke the cigarette to protect his life.

Still the pastor refused. Finally the prison guard said loudly so all the prisoners could hear him: "Do you see this man Jotham Mutebi? Do you see him?" All the prisoners thought he was going to announce his intention to kill the pastor as punishment for his refusal. Instead the guard said, "Do you see Jotham Mutebi? Don't touch him. I know now he is a true servant of God."

And a true servant of God he is. After his release from prison, he became a hero to Christians across Uganda. Later he served as the president of his church-planting organization, guiding hundreds of churches triumphantly through a season of severe trials and tribulations. Jotham Mutebi's life proves—as do the lives of David and Abraham Lincoln—that what we do in our caves matters. We must therefore develop "cave character" so that we can persevere when darkness descends around us. When we struggle to pay our bills, to stand by our marriages after unfaithfulness, or to heal fallouts with friends, we show people what we really believe about God.

## FLEE DARKNESS

When we face the darkness, our natural impulse is to take matters into our own hands. We want to eliminate the discomfort; we want to end the waiting period. We all know how David must have felt, but the lesson we learn from what he actually did is vital to living significant lives. In 1 Samuel 22,

David escaped to the cave of Adullam, which is about fifteen miles south-west of Jerusalem and worlds away from David's vision for his life:

> David left Gath and escaped to the cave of Adullam. When his brothers and his father's household heard about it, they went down to him there. All those who were in distress or in debt or discontented gathered around him, and he became their leader....
>
> But the prophet Gad said to David, "Do not stay in the stronghold. Go into the land of Judah." So David left and went to the forest of Hereth. (verses 1–2, 5)

What does this brief passage say to us today? I believe three lessons emerge here, three truths to remember when we're tempted to handle things our way instead of God's way: other people will be affected by my decision, some people will choose to follow my example, and God has a will concerning my actions.

The prophet Gad instructed David not to stay in the stronghold (the cave) but to go to the place where God had said his vision would become a reality. Now, I know it's not easy to remain visionary and alert to God's calling when we are afraid, bitter, or discouraged, but it's essential that we resist these dark, negative emotions so that God's purposes for us remain the goal of our pursuits *and* so that we lead the people closest to us in the right directions. Furthermore, if we make wrong decisions during our times of personal darkness, we're going to miss out on God's blessings. That's one reason why God wants us to be people of character inside and outside the cave, warriors whose lives give indisputable evidence that God is bigger than all our trials and disappointments.

## FACING FORGIVENESS

Another lesson we can take away from David's time as a "cave man" involves forgiveness. More specifically, David teaches us something about what it means to offer forgiveness in a spirit of love and grace, not because we are capable of doing so on our own, but because we experience God's outpouring of mercy on our own lives. When times are tough and you're struggling to remain obedient to God, you may find it incredibly challenging to show grace to others. When you have a bad day, it's much, much easier to kick the dog, blame others, hold grudges, and take out your hard feelings on those around you. But notice how David handled his bad day, so to speak.

Wedged between these verses is a hint about David's character. Specifically, notice that when David was in that cave, his family—the rejecting, belittling father and the doubting, scolding brother—came to his side. Talk about redemption. Their action definitely says something about David's character: some of the very people who had rejected him later chose to follow him when times were rough. And David didn't then exact justice on them. Instead, he helped them find safety:

> From there David went to Mizpah in Moab and said to the
> king of Moab, "Would you let my father and mother come
> and stay with you until I learn what God will do for me?"
> So he left them with the king of Moab, and they stayed with
> him as long as David was in the stronghold. (verses 3–4)

David had a golden opportunity to show his critics the door. He could have chosen right there to let King Saul loose on them. But he chose to allow God's nature to shine brighter than his darkness. *Character expresses God's love to others*—even to those who have hurt us.

And we do get hurt along this journey of life. So, while in church we sing about God "In the Sweet By and By," how many of us believe in God's nature and power in the nasty now and now? Faced with the chance to give his unsupportive family what they deserved, David instead gave them what they needed and what God had graciously offered him. David entered into a new relationship with them, a covenant triggered by forgiveness.

That kind of forgiveness is essential because we live in a broken world, and opportunities to extend forgiveness abound. Yet most hurting people have a hard time accepting and offering forgiveness. Maybe they never received it at home when they were growing up. Maybe they work in pressure cookers where people don't have even a second to lift their heads and affirm one another. Or maybe they're living out the psychiatrists' axiom that "hurt people hurt people." The sources of and reasons for all the hurt vary, but they all point to the fact that our churches need to be places where people are affirmed, forgiven, believed in, and helped. Often, those qualities are what attract new believers into church communities.

We can learn from David's example to extend forgiveness in all our dark trials—even to those who have hurt us—and thereby build community and trust. David moved one step closer to his destiny as king when he provided for his parents. God called him to be king because he knew David could do it. And God calls us to specific tasks because he knows that in his power we can do the jobs too.

## INTEGRITY INSPIRES

David not only forgave the people around him, but he began leading them (see 1 Samuel 22:2). He showed his faith in God by believing in God's dream for them even though they were distressed, indebted, and discontented.

The people in the cave recognized that David was different from their current king. David wasn't serving them to fulfill some personal agenda but to accomplish divine purposes.

Days later other men behold Saul's severe character deficit. When David was chased out of town, he'd asked Ahimelech the priest to give him the sword of Goliath and five loaves of bread from the Lord's temple. When Saul discovered that Ahimelech had done just what David requested, he called the priest's entire family (eighty-five men in total) before him and asked, "Why have you conspired against me?" The priest answered:

> Who of all your servants is as loyal as David, the king's son-in-law, captain of your bodyguard and highly respected in your household? Was that day [that he came to get food] the first time I inquired of God for him? Of course not! Let not the king accuse your servant or any of his father's family, for your servant knows nothing at all about this whole affair. (1 Samuel 22:13–15)

Listen to the reputation David built: he'd served faithfully, lived beyond reproach, and earned his reputation as a godly man. In fact, when Saul responded to Ahimelech's words by ordering his men to kill him and the other priests in his family, the soldiers refused. Get this: *David's integrity moved people to righteousness and affected the characters of people who knew him well.*

Remember these men serving in Saul's army had once been under David's command, and in time we'll see that many godly soldiers longed to be under David's command again. But for now, note David's approach when putting forth the effort wasn't easy. He didn't take the attitude, *I've been a high-ranking officer in Israel's army. It's below me to lead discouraged, defeated troops because I've led Israel's best.* Instead, David obeyed God and once again gave people what they needed.

So what causes people to serve God wholeheartedly? What causes individuals to do what is necessary to change the world? I believe the answer—in David's case and in yours and mine and anyone else's—is character. Godly character is explosive potential unleashed to change humanly unchangeable circumstances.

Can your marriage change? Can your family change? Can churches change communities? As I answer this third question for myself, I think about a pastor-friend of mine named Mark Crow. Mark came to be our youth pastor at Faith Family when I was thirty-one and he was thirty-four years old. He had already been a youth pastor in a megachurch and was being courted by others when he called me to offer his services. I didn't call him; he called me. He heard our church was growing, and he felt like God told him to make the offer.

We had a wonderful time together during perhaps the most formative years of our church. Then, when he was thirty-seven years old, Mark left Texas with his wife and four kids to plant a church in Oklahoma City. The only resources he had were his experience with God, a six-thousand-dollar gift from our church, his van, and his family. But Mark's an animated, high-energy guy—exciting to be around—and all of us at Faith Family knew that God had called the right guy for the job.

However, a week before Mark and his family were to leave, he and I were together when his phone rang. A few minutes into the conversation, I could see him heating up. His face got flushed, he kept shaking his head, and he walked in circles as he talked. Then he snapped the phone shut and came back: it was a call from his real estate agent in Oklahoma.

"These people have no character," Mark began. I knew that for a number of months, Mark had been going to Oklahoma. He had enlisted twenty-five people to help him start the church, and he had secured a building. He had made an offer, secured it with a handshake, and was waiting for the paperwork to be drawn up. But the real estate agent called to tell Mark that the agent representing the property had just struck up a deal with someone else. "I can't hire an attorney," Mark said. "There's nothing I can do!"

Now I'm sure that Mark isn't the only person who has felt what he felt that day. We are surrounded by people who don't hold our dreams dear. In fact, some people seem to get energized by making our efforts more difficult. The devil often gets in our way, and he doesn't seem to have a hard time finding people to join him. I've seen many a person stop at the cave en route to a significant life. There those people are somehow convinced that others control their destinies, and they quit. But other people don't control your destiny or mine. God controls it, and if you give God what he asks for, you will delight in what he gives back to you.

So what happened to Mark? Well, I knew Mark was a determined man, but this was a big blow. I asked him what he'd told the real estate agent. He said, "I told him I'm going to Oklahoma City, and when I get there, the sick are going to get healed and lives are going to change—and that will happen if I have a building or if I don't have a building. And I told them if I don't have a building, I'll go out in the city park. I'll use the bird bath as my pulpit, and I can do that because I'm a Crow. Either way, we're going to have a great church in Oklahoma!"

Today Mark has thousands of people in his church. Why? One reason is that Mark met his cave time with a character-based faith. Mark didn't blame others or curse his situation; rather he trusted God and obeyed.

During that time, he had twenty-five people looking at him, wondering what he was going to do. Those were not Mark's people—they were God's people. And Mark pursued God's vision and led the people well. Like David, Abraham Lincoln, and Jotham Mutebi, Mark Crow chose to exemplify the explosive power of our small acts of obedience.

# CHAPTER 5

## Don't Cave In

Imagine a woman—someone like your mother perhaps—riding a bus home after a long day at work. She's a hard-working, loving Christian with firm principles and deep compassion who is willing to stand on her feet all day to help support her family. As she sits back in her seat on the bus, resting her swollen and aching feet, a man approaches her. Clearly younger than she, he is able-bodied and in good health, yet he angrily demands that she give up her seat for him. She can't believe he would ask such a thing, but she begins to gather her purse and coat to relinquish her place.

But then something inside her shifts. She has had to do this far too many times, and today something is different. Not only is her body tired, but such poor treatment has made her spirit weary beyond measure. And she knows she's not alone. Thousands, if not millions, of other men and women like her are treated just as unfairly and often far worse. So she collapses back in her bus seat, looks the man in the eye, and tells him that she won't give up her seat. Her decision stuns the man and becomes the catalyst for an entire movement. Hundreds of people boycott the bus line, picket the local government, and become involved in a charge for national change.

The woman I just described was Rosa Parks. You probably know her story, but it's well worth remembering as we consider what it means to hold our ground as we pursue living significant lives. Like so many Americans at the time, Mrs. Parks knew in her heart that the segregation laws were unjust and unfair. But being conditioned to be an obedient, second-class citizen and to accept those laws, she allowed indecency to reign in the hearts of people who demanded she give up her bus seat or required her to use separate facilities when she went to the bathroom or needed a drink. But on that one significant day, something snapped inside her. Maybe she was simply so tired that she couldn't bear to yield once again to the absurdity of the situation and the segregation law behind it. So she acted on what she knew to be right even though she violated the law and risked her own safety.

Rosa Parks held her bus seat, held her ground, and quickly discovered that she personified what so many African Americans felt very deeply. Other voices quickly joined hers, including that of a young black pastor named Dr. Martin Luther King Jr. Mrs. Parks's simple decision to do what was right became the impetus for a nation-changing movement that restored human dignity. She is revered today as both a founder of the civil rights movement and a symbol of how one person, standing up for what he or she believes, can make a difference. She also exemplifies a truth that's foundational to significance: character is contagious, and people of character attract a crowd for right and important reasons.

Certainly Jesus Christ is our primary example of the power of character—the power of being and not just doing. Many of us have read "One Solitary Life," observations drawn from a sermon and later an essay credited to Dr. James A. Francis. As you read these motivating and thought-provoking words, try to identify the primary reason that Jesus has become the greatest life-giving figure in the history of the world:

> Here is a man who was born in an obscure village, the child
> of a peasant woman. He grew up in another village. He
> worked in a carpenter shop until He was thirty. Then for
> three years He was an itinerant preacher.
>
> He never owned a home. He never wrote a book. He
> never held an office. He never had a family. He never went
> to college. He never put His foot inside a big city. He never
> traveled two hundred miles from the place He was born. He
> never did one of the things that usually accompany greatness.
> *He had no credentials but Himself....*
>
> I am far within the mark when I say that all the armies
> that ever marched, all the navies that were ever built; all the
> parliaments that ever sat and all the kings that ever reigned,
> put together, have not affected the life of man upon this earth
> as powerfully as has that one solitary life.[*]

I include my italics here to identify what I believe to be the primary reason that Jesus pioneered an incomparable movement. Again, careful observation of the ministry of Jesus makes it clear that he understood the power of being and not just doing.

Think of Jesus's life. He did more than just talk about how the Sabbath

---

[*] Dr. James Allan Francis, "Jesus: A Brief Life," single sheet publication (Los Angeles: American Baptist Publication Society, circa 1930). An earlier version of the sermon by the same author was included under the title "Arise, Sir Knight!" in *The Real Jesus and Other Sermons* (Philadelphia: Judson Press, 1926), 123–4.

should benefit mankind. He asked his disciples to join him as he walked through the grain fields, picking some heads of grain. The Pharisees demanded an explanation asking, "Why are you doing what is unlawful on the Sabbath?" (Luke 6:2). That was exactly what Jesus wanted. Like Rosa Parks, Jesus knew it was time to stand his ground so people really looked. He hoped that God's law of grace and forgiveness, a law that gives life, would replace man's law, a law that had stolen life.

Jesus knew that standing up to powers that be and then enduring their persecution was necessary because doing so would highlight the importance of his message and empower people to act. Again and again in Scripture we read about him standing up to the Jewish leaders of his day. But Jesus didn't just talk about the need for religious professionals to live with the right motivations; Jesus overturned the moneychangers' tables and cleared out the temple. He didn't simply preach messages against prejudice (and, believe me, the Jews of his day were very prejudiced); Jesus went out of his way to help a Samaritan woman with questionable morals, Greek men who were seeking truth, and a Syrophoenician mother with a disturbed daughter. Jesus made his point very clear to his Jewish disciples: they were God's chosen people but not his *only* people.

We don't have enough space to mention all the times Jesus communicated what needed to be said by what he did. However, let me share a couple more that I love. When Jesus risked his life in a terrible storm at sea in order to minister to people, what was he saying? "If you want to help people like this get truly free, you better be willing to endure a few storms." When Jesus appeared again and again to his fearful, unstable disciples after his resurrection, what was he saying? "I am not just telling you that you need to love one another even as I have loved you. I am making sure you know what real love is."

## CHARACTER AND COMPANIONS

At this point you may be thinking, *What does all this have to do with me? I don't see myself as a Rosa Parks, Dr. Martin Luther King Jr., King David, the apostle Paul, and certainly not Jesus Christ!* No, but let me ask you to consider something important: what will people remember about you?

Causes worth embracing surround all of us every day, but I've learned that *someone has to demonstrate that something is worth doing before others join in the doing.* That's why character is at the heart of the pursuit of a significant life. Remember that character is doing the right thing regardless—even when it is unpopular and difficult.

And consider how teams that make this world a better place to live are formed. Isn't it usually after a person of character attracts people to a cause worth achieving? As people come together, their combined talents turn that dream into a reality.

I believe Jesus Christ never went to college, wrote a book, had a family, or held an office because he was trying to teach us that ministry is first about *being* and then about *doing.* After all, as the body of Christ, we have the privilege of releasing his presence into the lives of people everywhere as we embrace our God-given causes.

Let me return to David, the central character of our study and a man whose life clearly illustrates the Cs—or seeds, as I like to call them—that grow a significant life. In 1 Samuel 22, we find a touching story that I believe reveals one reason why people willingly signed on with their lives to God's dream and David's vision.

By the end of 1 Samuel 22, Saul had killed Ahimelech and nearly all of his family for supporting David. However, one of Ahimelech's sons—Abiathar—escaped and paid a visit to David. He told David that Saul had killed eighty-five of the Lord's priests. Listen to these words spoken by David to a man who had lost his whole family:

> I am responsible for the death of your father's whole family.
> Stay with me; don't be afraid; the man who is seeking your
> life is seeking mine also. You will be safe with me. (1 Samuel
> 22:22–23)

People accepting responsibility and bearing our sorrows with us, comfort, safety, vision—these are some of the things we are all looking for, aren't they? We all have scars, so we're attracted to people whose compassion acts in ways that make our world a better place.

Now think for a moment about power and character. Power can turn people's heads for a moment of amazement, but character can join people's hearts for a lifetime. We naturally seek out people who have the power to make our lives better, but we stay closely connected to people who not only have the power we need but also hearts we can trust.

I remember one unforgettable father-son campout in the early days of our church. We fathers used our talents to design eighteen hours worth of entertaining and enjoyable events: cookouts, capture-the-flag competitions, outdoor devotions, and an obstacle course. But the weather didn't cooperate, and our plans were doused as quickly as the campfire. It turned cold and rainy, and we scrambled to plan new "waterproof" events. I don't recall all of the new events we planned, but I'll never forget that weekend— nor will my son Michael. We dads could've justifiably accepted defeat, but we delighted in going the extra mile to create spontaneous fun. Our sons were bonded to us in deeper ways because they saw how much we cared about them.

Isn't that what Abiathar sensed when he interacted with David? Yes, and this is a crucial lesson for all of us trying to live significantly: *when we solve problems that matter to others, we create partners.* Acting on this truth can start the healing process between disengaged spouses, with distanced children, or among divided church members. I recently heard survey results that revealed the following: 90 percent of American adults want a lifelong stable marriage, yet less than 50 percent of American adults experience a stable marriage. I believe one reason is because stable marriages require two people who each choose to cultivate a godly character and live it out in their relationships. It takes that kind of character to bridge the distance between parents and children and to unify divided churches too!

Character focuses on who we all must be to create a better world. But before God could empower David and his companions to create a better Israel, he had to convince them all to become better people and better partners with one another. Partnerships have a profound effect on how we behave and pursue our God-given purposes.

## PARTNERSHIPS EQUAL POWER

Friends matter when times are the darkest. Just think back to dark times that you have overcome, and my guess is that you'll picture hovering over you the faces of those who helped you greatly and whom you love dearly.

That was certainly true of David: his need for the people around him deepened his sense of appreciation for them. Like many of us, he learned that some of the treasures of dark times are the lessons we learn and the friendships we form or strengthen during those difficult days. I suppose it's an insight David passed on to Solomon, his son and the nation's next king.

Under Solomon's reign, Israel exploded with wealth and prosperity, which was made possible only because of a great God's ability and Solomon's partnership with godly people. Read what Solomon wrote near the end of his life:

> Two are better than one,
>> because they have a good return for their work:
> If one falls down,
>> his friend can help him up.
> But pity the man who falls
>> and has no one to help him up!
> Also, if two lie down together, they will keep warm.
>> But how can one keep warm alone?
> Though one may be overpowered,
>> two can defend themselves.
> A cord of three strands is not quickly broken.
>> (Ecclesiastes 4:9–12)

Clearly, Solomon understood the benefits of partnership. As an older man, he had experienced firsthand the importance of keeping talented people of character around him. This wise man's insight masterfully unveils the fourfold blessing God wants to give us through partnership.

First off, *partnership enables prosperity.* When people join their skills together, they can accomplish more than if they act alone. Rosa Parks accomplished more because of Dr. Martin Luther King Jr., and all of us accomplish more when we join ourselves to the right team. At Faith Family Church, we often say that we would rather be a small part of something big for God than a big part of something small.

Second, *partnership provides protection.* We all need people who have our backs, as the saying goes. Whether we like it or not, an evil world will hit us from time to time, and we will fall. That's when we're grateful for a friend who picks us up.

Third, *partnership fuels passions.* It's easy for disappointing events and painful trials to turn our hearts cold and sap our energy. If something isn't done, we can die inside. Fellowship is God's plan for keeping us warm and alive inside.

Finally, *partnership brings power.* God describes great partnerships as a cord. An old cowboy illustrated this by showing me his calving rope and explaining that all strands of a rope break somewhere. But ropes bind strands together so that when one strand breaks, another has the power to hold the rope together. I think that's why God sent Moses with Aaron, why he paired Joshua and Caleb, and why Jesus sent his disciples out two by two.

And that's why God calls us to build quality partnerships before we need them, so we will be there for one another when the need does arise. The importance of partnership may not be obvious to us all the time, but if you think back over your life, you will plainly see that you do need other people. (We *all* do!)

I like the story about the CEO of a large insurance company who goes back to his wife's hometown for her high-school reunion. The fuel tank is empty, so they pull into a gas station, the attendant comes out, and the CEO goes inside to pay.

When he comes out, he sees his wife gabbing away with the attendant, and it turns out, he hears as he walked by, that the two dated in high school and were catching up on old times. So the big shot CEO lets his wife talk as he gets into the car and gives her plenty of time to get in. As they drive away, the CEO smiles at her and says, "Just think. If you hadn't married me, you would be married to that gas pumper." His wife smiles back at him and replies, "No, *you* just think. If I had married him, you'd be pumping gas, and he'd be a CEO."

Overcomers who accomplish great things learn to appreciate their allies along the way. They know that great tasks take teamwork, so don't overlook the people God has placed in your life. Together, you can become who he designed you to be and accomplish what he wants you to do

## PARTNERSHIPS EQUAL PERSEVERANCE

David Swann is a dear friend who pastors a church in Clovis, New Mexico. He is also one of the founders of the Significant Church Network, and he serves there as a vice president. His church currently ministers to about two thousand people in weekly services, and that number is about 4 percent of their county's population. The church has also ministered to 10 percent of the county's high-school students through various avenues of ministry. But it hasn't been an easy road.

For ten years, David's church couldn't grow beyond two hundred people. His heart grew heavy, and he was ready to move to another city. I love hearing his wife, Roxanne, tell of his struggles because wives never sugarcoat it, do they? She explained to me how David came to her days before the tenth-anniversary celebration of their church. The president of the Bible school they had graduated from was scheduled to speak, and the congregation's excitement was growing as the anniversary weekend neared.

But David shared some news with Roxanne that extinguished the excitement for her. He said, "The Sunday after the anniversary service, honey, I'm going to tell the church I'm done. We've finished our work here." Roxanne said it felt as if someone had told her she was getting divorced while on her honeymoon.

But ultimately David didn't quit. Instead he was strengthened to "grow on" because he had a great partner in his wife. And isn't that what all of us need? I'm thinking of people in dreamless places—in an abusive home, a draining relationship, a seemingly dead-end workplace filled with heartless people. Where do we find the strength to go on? The biblical account of King David shows us that we can find strength in our partnerships with God and with competent, caring people of character who are committed to seeing us through our darkest times.

In 1 Samuel 23 we see those kinds of people in David's life. King Saul had ordered all his forces to Keilah to besiege David and his men. Keilah was a town with gates and bars, and Saul concluded that he could capture David there because he would have no means of escape (see verses 7–8).

However, one of David's trusted friends helped the future king escape. Here's what happened:

> When David learned that Saul was plotting against him, he
> said to Abiathar the priest, "Bring the ephod." (verse 9)

The ephod was a four-colored piece of clothing God instructed the priest to wear whenever he was asking for God's perspective. The gold color symbolized heaven's supremacy; the blue, honor and exaltation coming from above; the purple, the royal status of God's children; and the scarlet, God's sacrifice providing redemption. I'm sure it was a very helpful reminder and call to prayer for David.

And a new perspective certainly paid off for David. He escaped Saul's trap and entered into the next stage of his significant life—just as David Swann did after his wife helped him find a new perspective on his pastorate.

Instead of moving to another city, David Swann let God move in his heart. God led him to establish another productive partnership, this one with a successful pastor who cared about other pastors. David attended his conferences, bought his tapes, and worked through the process of maturing as a pastor. When friends scoffed at the investment he was making, David responded, "If you think education is expensive, try ignorance. It threatens our futures every day and keeps our dreams from coming true." Now everyone who knows David easily sees that he has become who he is through partnerships that enabled prosperity, provided protection, fueled passions, and brought power. And the exciting thing is he is now doing for others what was done for him.

## Partnerships Equal Priorities

You and I can surprise our world just as David did, but it won't happen if our hearts are indifferent during those dark times when we must nevertheless make right choices. What if Rosa Parks, David Swann, or—most significantly—Jesus himself had remained indifferent to our great needs and made other choices?

Their decisions weren't easy. Whether we like it or not, the Enemy will constantly attack us if we are pursuing worthwhile dreams. And we better be ready because it will happen whether we feel ready or not.

In 1 Samuel 23, David escaped from Keilah and went to the desert strongholds of Ziph to hide. But to David's dismay, Saul did not give up his search for him. In fact, David learned that Saul wanted to take his life (see 1 Samuel 23:14–15). At this point David needed another courageous partner of character.

> And Saul's son Jonathan went to David…and helped him
> find strength in God. "Don't be afraid," he said. "My father
> Saul will not lay a hand on you. You will be king over Israel,
> and I will be second to you. Even my father Saul knows this."
> (1 Samuel 23:16–17)

What an amazing friend Jonathan showed himself to be. In essence he said, "God is choosing the man with greatest character to be king of Israel, and that's who I want to work for." This is a critical part of character. When we find a person of character in difficult circumstances, our job as God's people is to get that person through the tough times.

For you see, it hadn't take long for Saul's son—and all of Israel—to see the difference between David and Saul that God saw.

Saul fought *against* everyone while David fought *for* everyone.

Saul fought for *his* pleasures while David fought for *God's* purposes.

My late father-in-law, Pastor John Osteen, was my mentor, my pastor, and like a second father to me. Not only did he build a megachurch with ten thousand people back in the day when megachurches were rare, but he was the pastor to thousands of pastors across America and around the world. One day he told me a story I will never forget because it illustrates so clearly how the greatest among us still need help along the way.

At the time, he was in his midseventies and nearing the end of his exemplary life. He and my mother-in-law, Dodie, had driven to Victoria to spend the day with my family and me. The week before, he had preached in an anniversary service at the church he had pastored forty years earlier when he was in his early thirties. He had suffered an unwanted divorce during that time and felt that perhaps his circumstances disqualified him for ministry—and some people agreed.

With tears in his eyes, my father-in-law said, "Jim, do you know what I preached about at the anniversary service? The woman with the alabaster box who anointed Jesus before his crucifixion and burial. The perfume reminded Jesus that she loved him and believed in him as the Pharisees condemned him, the outside world criticized him, and the Romans crucified him. I told the people they were like the woman with the alabaster box to me. All I have accomplished has only been done because their belief in me urged me on, and everywhere I have gone the beautiful memory of their love has been with me."

Wow! There were tears in my eyes now as well. But he had more to say: "Jim, if I had only known during that trying time that God planned on bringing Dodie and my five children and the people of Lakewood Church into my future, I would have never entertained quitting the ministry. Continuing on in God's plan would have been easy then."

Character counts—our character and the character of the people we surround ourselves with. Character affects all of our choices. Our unconditional love and belief in one another will make all of our lives better. So let's seek out good partners and concentrate on being good partners, and together we'll have worthy people to help along the way!

# CHAPTER 6

## *Build on Bedrock*

You remember the type. There was one in every class: straight As, teacher's pet, led a Bible study in church, played first chair in the band, worked in the family business, and was probably going to be a millionaire. Everyone considered that person the most likely to succeed—and then some. *He's perfect,* we thought as we wistfully compared ourselves to him. And we've all had problems following those whose lives look better than ours.

But then we get to know him: he was actually not his father's favorite son, his brothers didn't really like him, and he played the harp because that was what the boss wanted him to do. He was pushed out of his job, forced to leave his wife, and threatened at knifepoint. He had some serious in-law troubles; some of his relatives were responsible for several gangland murders—of *priests!* As a result, this person who seemed to have the ideal life actually ended up living for some time in places we would never want to go. Now he was leading a small army of stragglers, and we're all certain he never dreamed of leading *them*. Given the chance, he would've undoubtedly gone back to work for the king because, at heart, he was a servant.

This man was doing his duty to God and his country—obeying the law and leading an army. But those he was leading were not fully aware of their potential, so David's passion became showing them what people living for the right reasons could accomplish. They started winning—knocking those Philistines out of the Israelite town—but the town accepted the victory, then betrayed them, sending them packing back to the caves.

Such is the stuff a significant life is made of. *We must passionately embrace what is right to do even when the situation seems to indicate that our actions won't matter.*

## WALK A MILE

What happens when we climb in someone else's shoes: the world takes on a different perspective, doesn't it? This season of David's life illustrates just how essential convictions are in times of chaos. Despite extreme pressure, David enabled distressed soldiers to become successful soldiers: six hundred Israelites learned under David's leadership that God doesn't create people to fail; rather it is wrong principles that fail us. That's why embracing God's principles turns curses into blessing—in marriages, homes, churches, communities, nations. David showed his men—and us—a better way.

And we need that better way. Distress and heartbreak fill our world. As a result, people crave enjoyable lives, meaningful relationships, and significance. But our quest for these things is backward: too often, we try to fix our lives by sheer willpower, and we continue to allow the wrong people to have a say in our lives. Instead, if we would just choose to live by God's principles and to be involved in right relationships, the blessings God has in store for us might appear sooner than we think.

To clarify my point, let me tell you a story about a woman I know named Isabel. Early in my ministry, when life was really crazy with both my new church and my family growing fast, Isabel used to come over and help my wife, Tamara, around the house. Isabel displayed a beautiful servant's heart: to me, to my family, and especially to God.

Suddenly, though, the unexpected happened: Isabel's husband unjustly accused her of wrongdoing and divorced her. Needless to say, she was devastated, and for many weeks the toll on her life was very obvious. Oh, she still served God, but not in the same way she had before the divorce. We knew her heart was broken, but there wasn't much we could do. Her husband had believed a lie, he was gone, and that was that—for most people anyway. But not Isabel. After about a month, I saw something change in her.

She never said it outright, but I watched as she came to grips with the situation and started zealously serving the Lord again. In fact, I soon saw her serving God even more fervently than before. Also, she was more aware of other people's pain, and she became intent on making a difference in the life of every hurting person she met. Simply put, she put on the garment of praise, and our congregation watched with joy as the light came back into her eyes. It was so beautiful to see how this incredible woman found her joy restored despite her incredible loss.

One Sunday night I was greeting people from the platform at church, and I saw Isabel dart across the sanctuary with the focus of an Olympic sprinter. I thought somebody must have cracked his or her head open and kindhearted Isabel was hurrying to help. Then I saw her come to a halt before a handsome guy who had just entered our church. *A relative,* I thought. *Maybe someone she invited to church.*

The next day when Isabel came to the house to help Tamara, I asked her about that man. She told me she had definitely noticed the handsome man but that he was no relative. She explained, "Pastor, you taught us that according to the Bible, faith without works is dead. When I saw that man, I knew I had to act on my faith." Isabel explained how God had opened her heart to the possibility of dating again. To make a long story short, Isabel and that handsome visitor are happily married. They never could have children, so they adopted their beloved Jeremiah.

Now I respect Isabel for many reasons, but what I respect most is her decision to continue living by faith after another person's mistake brought chaos into her life. Remember that *character is doing right regardless,* and that kind of character has the power to transform lives.

In light of that truth, think about fixing more than your hair in the morning. You and I can also fix our attitudes and characters and positively impact others' lives. Unfortunately, I'm afraid a lot of hurting people were never taught that we all lose valuable things or that everybody's heart feels overwhelmed in the face of overpowering circumstances. But it's at those chapters in our lives that we show our true characters. Some of us start complaining: "If God really loved me, he would never let this happen," "All I am is a maid," "No matter what I do, this situation won't turn around." Some of us start condemning: "Where are my friends when I need them?" "That pastor never came to see me," "The church is just a bunch of hypocrites."

It will serve us better to remember that no matter how much other people want to help us during the hard times, we ourselves must exercise faith if we are to walk through the darkness. The book of Proverbs teaches,

"As [a man] thinks in his heart, so is he" (Proverbs 23:7, NKJV). This truth means that the dream I hold on to in my heart each day is what my life will become tomorrow.

And I know, oftentimes, circumstances seem to confirm that God is allowing our Enemy to slap us around like punching bags. That's when we must remember that God has told us to stand firm and has promised that standing firm would bring his blessings into our futures.

Also, our own humanness can trip us up and compromise our tomorrows. Assuming that David was a man of steel, for example, would be wrong. In fact, the Bible makes sure we see that he was a fallible person. Like you and me, David was very capable of having his humanity interfere with his calling. But his mistakes compelled him to live just like Isabel—working out his salvation with fear and trembling (see Philippians 2:12).

## KNOW YOUR REAL BATTLES

David lived a life of righteousness, but still everything seemed to turn out wrong. Just like Isabel, David did all he knew to do—only to be disappointed by the outcome. In 1 Samuel 24, we find Saul still in hot pursuit of David, chasing him from cave to cave in the mountains.

> Saul took three thousand chosen men from all Israel and set out to look for David and his men near the Crags of the Wild Goats.
>
> He came to the sheep pens along the way; a cave was there, and Saul went in to relieve himself. David and his men were far back in the cave. The men said, "This is the

day the LORD spoke of when he said to you, 'I will give your enemy into your hands for you to deal with as you wish.'" (verses 2–4)

There it is—the opportunity everyone was waiting for. David could show Saul once and for all who was boss, and all of Israel would be able to rejoice, knowing that their new king capitalized on his opportunity. But David saw the situation differently, and he merely "cut off a corner of Saul's robe" (verse 4). Even so, the Bible says that David was "conscience-stricken" (verse 5). He said to all his men, "The LORD forbid that I should do such a thing to my master, the LORD's anointed, or lift my hand against him" (verse 6).

Now fast forward several thousand years. If David were running for president of the United States, what would we say about him? Would we call him the comeback kid? Would we praise him as a man of conscience? A unifier rather than a divider? Or would we call him a wimp? We Americans like to take things into our own hands, to control our own destinies, and to pull ourselves up by our bootstraps. We like a good fight, and we appreciate when one person turns the tables on another.

As I've said, though, David saw things differently: public opinion didn't matter because David served God; Saul's past didn't matter because David lived redemptively, not vengefully; David could have killed Saul but didn't because his character mattered more to him than convenience. So, instead of carrying out his followers' wishes, David acted according to his conscience, which enabled him to act according to God's will. As a person of character David recognized that a wicked culture can't be overcome by copying or conforming to its ways and that instead a superior culture must be modeled in hopes that one day it will be followed. The apostle Paul said as much to the Roman Christians suffering because of the godless culture in which they lived: "Do not be overcome by evil, but overcome evil with good" (12:21).

But the ugly truth remains: sometimes all the right heavenly motives seem to amount to no earthly good, and we are tempted to bring about change by earthly means.


## THE POWER OF OBEDIENCE

In the 1940s a man named Clarence Jordan founded Koinonia Farm in Americus, Georgia. Dr. Jordan was a man of unusual ability and character. He had two PhDs, one in agriculture and one in Greek and Hebrew. So gifted was he that he could have chosen to do anything he wanted—and he chose to serve the poor.

Koinonia Farm served both poor whites and poor blacks. As you might guess, such an idea did not go over well in the Deep South at that time. Ironically, much of the resistance came from church people who followed the unjust laws of segregation as strictly as the other folks in town did.

The townspeople tried everything to stop Clarence. They slashed car tires when workers drove into town, and they boycotted his produce. This kind of pressure was ever-present for fourteen years. Finally, in 1954, the Ku Klux Klan had had enough of Clarence Jordan, so they decided to get rid of him once and for all. They came one night with guns and torches and set fire to every building on the farm except Clarence's home, which they riddled with bullets. They chased off all the families except one black family who refused to leave.

Clarence recognized the voices of many of the Klansmen, and, as you might guess, some of them were church people. Another was a local newspaper reporter. The next day that reporter came out to see what remained of the farm. The rubble still smoldered and the land was scorched, but he found Clarence hoeing and planting in the field. "I heard the awful news," he called to Clarence, "and I came out to do a story on the tragedy of your farm closing."

Clarence just kept on hoeing and planting. The reporter kept prodding and poking, trying to disturb this quietly determined man who was obviously planting instead of packing his bags. Finally, the reporter said in a haughty voice, "Well, Dr. Jordan, you got two PhDs, and you've put fourteen years into this farm, and now there's nothing left of it at all. Just how successful do you think you've been?"

Clarence stopped hoeing. Turning his penetrating eyes on the reporter, he spoke quietly but firmly: "About as successful as the Cross." Jordan continued, "Sir, I don't think you understand us. What we are about is not success but faithfulness. We're staying. Good day." Clarence and his partners rebuilt Koinonia, and the farm is going strong to this day.

People who live significant lives—people like King David and Clarence Jordan—force us to reconsider our views on weakness and strength. I certainly appreciate the value of having the power necessary to fight back (strength), but the ability to fight back doesn't necessarily mean it's the best choice or God's will, does it? I know I've turned messes into bigger messes by fighting back in my own power, and I'm guessing you have too. Even when I seemingly won the argument or fight, I later learned that I had lost something much more valuable—a person's affection, the team's loyalty, or the favor that would have paid greater dividends.

Now, up until this point, David had done a pretty exemplary job demonstrating to his men that weakness is not an unwillingness to act.

Rather, weakness is acting in a way that sabotages our impact for God. David still looked like the golden boy, but even a person of David's character can crumble if enough pressure mounts—and pressure was mounting.

In 1 Samuel 25, we read that Samuel died. David's mentor was no longer available to him even as his troubles continued. All of Israel assembled to mourn the prophet's passing—all of Israel except David, who was still on King Saul's Most Wanted list.

Not long after that, it was festival time in Israel (probably Passover), and David was still in the desert. Any of us who have ever been kept from getting home at Christmastime know how David must have felt. Those times were very bad for David: he was living like a vagabond, he had lost his mentor, he was barred from the funeral, and he couldn't get home for the holidays.

At that point he heard that a local farmer was shearing some sheep, and he sent his men with a message: "Tell him, look, we've been out in your fields for a long time. We didn't mistreat your shepherds or steal your sheep. Ask your servants and they will tell you. We love the Lord, and we want to honor Him. We also want to celebrate, but can't without your assistance, so our master asked if we could have some of your sheep and bread" (see verses 7–8).

Nabal was the owner of the sheep, and he was a grouch—a very wealthy grouch, in fact, who owned a thousand goats and three thousand sheep. Listen to what Nabal said:

> Nabal answered David's servants, "Who is this David? Who is
> this son of Jesse? Many servants are breaking away from their
> masters these days. Why should I take my bread and water,
> and the meat I have slaughtered for my shearers, and give it
> to men coming from who knows where?" (verse 11)

Nabal didn't realize whom he was dealing with or the kinds of military victories David had to his credit. Nabal also seemed to have forgotten that when a needy person with a good reputation begged to be part of the Lord's celebration, you wouldn't gain respect or allies by turning that person away.

In Nabal's case, he said the wrong thing at the wrong time, and David seemed to have a testosterone attack. "Put on your swords!" David commanded. The narration continues, "About four hundred men went up with David, while two hundred stayed with the supplies" (verse 13).

David's response shouldn't surprise us. It doesn't matter who we are or what our work is, enough pressure makes us vulnerable, and eventually we are worn down and weakened. And when we are weak, we are capable of making decisions that sabotage our lives. Even our most respected leaders (or perhaps *especially* our most respected leaders) often live at dangerous emotional levels and can act rashly.

## ARM YOURSELF WITH ALLIES

The temptation to act impulsively is yet another reason why God calls us to build relationships with proven people of character. President Ronald Reagan once observed, "The greatest sound that a man hears is the sound of footsteps coming to meet him at the door." Even the most powerful people in the world need to know someone they trust is waiting to strengthen them, and these powerful people must choose their allies wisely.

In this case—without David even knowing it—Nabal's wife, Abigail, interceded on behalf of her husband:

> Abigail lost no time. She took two hundred loaves of bread,
> two skins of wine, five dressed sheep, five seahs of roasted

grain, a hundred cakes of raisins and two hundred cakes of pressed figs, and loaded them on the donkeys. (verse 18)

Then she got on her own donkey and rode out to see David herself. In chapter 5 we discussed the importance of godly partnerships, and here is a perfect example of why we need to be surrounded by people of character. When Abigail encountered David, she humbled herself before this man who was intent on the sword. Hear what she said:

> "My lord, let the blame be on me alone. Please let your serv-
> ant speak to you; hear what your servant has to say. May my
> lord pay no attention to that wicked man Nabal.... His name
> is Fool, and folly goes with him." (verses 24–25)

Abigail went before David and begged that he pardon her husband. She recognized what Nabal didn't: basically, that whoever lives by the sword dies by it. Consequently, she was wise enough to protect her husband from himself.

This situation reminds me of a scene in *Braveheart,* one of my favorite movies. William Wallace is walking through the forest on a scouting mission. Behind him is an enemy scout that he is not aware of. All of a sudden, a man holding an ax pops up in front of him. Wallace is sure the man is an enemy because he obviously belongs to a Celtic tribe—and everyone knows the Celts are crazy. But Wallace cannot ready himself to fight before the man throws his weapon in Wallace's direction. Wallace ducks, and the weapon strikes Wallace's real enemy behind him. It turns out that the man in front of Wallace, who should have been an enemy, is actually an ally, and that the man following him, who should have been a friend, is actually an enemy.

Has something like that ever happened to you? Has an apparent enemy ever turned out to be a friend—or vice versa? If so, then you know the value of having people with godly character watching your back.

## DARKNESS INTO LIGHT

We must remember that fulfilled dreams require us to obey wise principles even when it isn't exciting to do so. David, my friend Isabel, and Clarence Jordan all illustrate the important lesson that God's principles work just as he promised they would—and they work for all types of people in very different places.

David knew how important managing his character was when making choices under pressure. That's why, when he wrote his last song as Israel's psalmist, after the Lord delivered him from all his enemies, including Saul, he was able to declare:

> The LORD has rewarded me according to my righteousness,
>     according to my cleanness in his sight.
>
> To the faithful you show yourself faithful,
>     to the blameless you show yourself blameless,
> to the pure you show yourself pure,
>     but to the crooked you show yourself shrewd.
> You save the humble,
>     but your eyes are on the haughty to bring them low.
>         (2 Samuel 22:25–28)

It's hard to live in this world without an evil, unclean thought ever affecting our hearts. But we must keep our hands clean in God's sight if our God in heaven is going to reward our lives on earth. But it's sometimes easier to pull out a sword than it is to obey God's Spirit. A sword gets rid of the problem right away, but we better be careful because the sword usually replaces it with a greater problem. We all have both the sword and God's Spirit at our disposal, and wise people surround themselves with friends who help them choose the Spirit when they are at dangerous emotional levels.

In Abigail, David saw a person who understood the importance of acting according to God's nature. By doing so, she displayed exactly what David needed when, in a moment of weakness, he nearly fell on his face by choosing the sword. That's why, after Nabal's death, David asked her to become his teammate (see 1 Samuel 25:39).

By the way, scholars commenting on this period of David's life say that if David had killed either Saul or Nabal, there is a great chance his own men would have killed him. That thought is based on a mistake David later made, a mistake that negatively affected their lives, and they spoke of stoning him (see 1 Samuel 30:6).

Slowly but surely, David was being prepared to lead a significant life as king, wasn't he? In his youth, he learned the value of facing trials with confidence. Perhaps his life inspired the author of the epistle to the Hebrews to encourage us all: "So do not throw away your confidence; it will be richly rewarded" (10:35).

Now as the internal battle raged, David chose character, and God taught him that character is the armor overcomers must fight with. Look closely at the next two verses from the scripture I shared earlier, a passage celebrating the power of character.

> You are my lamp, O LORD;
>> the LORD turns my darkness into light.
> With your help I can advance. (2 Samuel 22:29–30)

So let me ask you a few questions. What cave are you in? Is the darkness scaring you? Are you letting God have his way in your heart and in your life? And have you surrounded yourself with friends who understand the danger you're facing?

If you focus on what God has given you as well as on his promises, then you can take heart, knowing that you will emerge from your cave as a victor. As David himself expressed it, "*I would have lost heart,* unless I had believed that I would see the goodness of the LORD in the land of the living. Wait on the LORD; be of good courage, and He shall strengthen your heart" (Psalm 27:13–14, NKJV).

Character is crucial to who we are deep down and how we make choices every day. *When we realize that God created us with unique abilities, preferences, and giftings, then we can move boldly beyond the caves that we find ourselves in.* We will be able to act on who we are as his son or daughter, empowered by his truth and determined to fulfill our eternal potential.

# PART III

# Concentration

*I will praise the LORD, who counsels me;*
*even at night my heart instructs me.*
*I have set the LORD always before me.*
*Because he is at my right hand,*
*I will not be shaken.*

PSALM 16:7–8

# CHAPTER 7

# Side Tracks

My family, perhaps like yours, enjoys watching classic Christmas movies during the holiday season. One of our favorites is *It's a Wonderful Life* with the lovable Jimmy Stewart as George Bailey, a man in a soul-threatening bind who discovers that being content isn't conditional on how much money you have, but rather on the love of friends and family. Even though I would question some of the movie's theology (I'm just not sure about that angel merit system!), the story reminds us to pay attention to what we've been given and how we pour out our lives for others. I like it because it reminds us that each one of us is significant, no matter where we live, no matter how small our circles of influence, or no matter what conditions our peers are in. The story reminds us to hang on tightly to our faith even when our lives get sidetracked.

When I saw that film recently, my heart warmed with thoughts of my friend Pat Butcher who lives in a small town in eastern Kentucky. Like George Bailey, he grew up in the same town where he now works. The townspeople know his name, they know his family, and they know his past. Pat went away to school, had a heart to travel, and saw himself exploring an exciting career that would take him around the world. However, he quickly found himself back in Kentucky working on his family's pig farm. "I came back," he says, "because I really didn't know what I wanted to do. And because my brother and family were still farming, I felt like I had some farm debts to pay."

Pat never dreamed that his significant life would be lived out in serving the people he grew up with. After all, Pat knew he had changed while away at college, but their lives hadn't changed much. Pat didn't feel he was better than they were, just different, and he wasn't sure his old friends were ready to accept who he had become. And, as we all know, there's no place to hide in a small town.

After being home for a while, a local church heard that Pat was back in town and invited him to come and speak. The members liked him so much that they asked him to be their pastor, and he agreed to stay for a year. Suddenly, Pat was traveling all right, but only one county over, not around the world like he had once dreamed. Though the idea of being a pastor had crossed his mind, he wasn't sure that was what he was called to do, but nonetheless he continued to serve.

After his year at the church, Pat found himself once again back on the pig farm working with his family. Still not knowing what he should do, Pat started a Bible study at his house. The study slowly grew until it eventually needed a new place to meet. It was becoming clearer and clearer that God wanted Pat to shepherd this small body of believers. With a stronger sense of direction, Pat began looking for a place for the group to meet, and he

soon found a space where they could continue to grow. "I signed a five-year lease for a storefront," Pat told me. Even though he didn't have a large enough congregation with the necessary resources to pay for the facility, Pat had a plan. "I was going to pay for it with my pigs."

A few days later, though, a storm kicked up and dropped several inches of rain in less than an hour. Floods surged throughout the town. Worried about his pigs, Pat drove out to the farm and saw his father standing there. "I got some bad news," his father told him. "It started to flood, and your pigs ran to their nests. I'm afraid they all drowned, Son."

Let's stop here for a minute. What would *you* do if you were in Pat's situation? You just signed a lease, the bill collectors will come sooner than later, and your source of income just got washed off the face of the earth. Have you ever been there? Maybe your mortgage payment was coming due, you couldn't pay an electric bill, or your kids needed medicine just after the furnace broke? Consider how you typically respond when your own pigs are lost in a flood.

It can be so tempting during the floods of life to lose heart. Even those of us with the strongest faith can quickly feel like giving up when life beats us down. In times of trouble, I've seen people come to all sorts of conclusions. They blame God, they get depressed because life has turned against them, or they simply check out because nothing is going their way.

To double the trouble, what happens if you're like Pat—or George Bailey—and your dreams for yourself are just not coming true? What do you do when your life gets sidetracked from the route you imagined yourself traveling? How do you feel when the future you dreamed of dies or is in desperate need of life support? We had plans for international adventures and exciting experiences, but instead we're right back where we started—working a pig farm in a no-name town.

As we saw in the previous section, sometimes we—like David—can't leave our caves no matter how hard we try, and we lose heart as we look for the light at the end of the tunnel. Maybe our friends married well, but we're still single. Maybe our high-school classmates went to college, moved to the big city, and became successful. Maybe someone else has children while we don't. We can find lots of reasons to feel like we haven't made anything of ourselves, and that's just about the time something else goes wrong and makes us wonder if trying to improve our circumstances is even worth the effort.

Well, there's an important lesson about significance to be learned here. My friend Pat expressed it well: "If you're going to serve God, there are going to be a few trials along the way. At those moments when you're left staring at a drowned pig, the Lord wants to see if you're really on board." That's what faith is all about. And *faith is the mortar that holds the cornerstones of confidence and character in place despite the shifting sands and high tides of life.* We can often feel like we're living on the side tracks of life rather than on the routes we had imagined for ourselves, but we must trust that God will still guide us to our destinations. Faith allows us to adapt to the unexpected and unwanted circumstances without giving up on God and his plan.

Although these desperate situations are incredibly difficult and even painful, they can become a refiner's fire for significance. When our back is against the wall, we often realize we have nowhere else to turn, and we fall on our knees. During those times when we lack the necessary talent or resources, we learn just how trustworthy God truly is. Pat, for instance, realized that if it's God will, it's God's bill. The Lord told him, *Never look to those pigs to be your source of provision.*

Pat's problem was not resolved immediately, but his story is typical of significant people who learn to trust God in the most trying of times. No matter how confident we are, no matter how much character we've got, life sometimes gets crazy, and we can get off track. When we do, we have to remember that God's vision is afforded by his divine resources while our vision is enabled only by human capital. That fact makes it easy to get on board.

## God's Economy

There was a time in American history when the steam engine was the symbol of American prosperity. Its versatility brought booming economic growth, and with that growth came an entirely new standard of living in our country. With railroads in place for the steam-driven engines, durable goods could get from one part of the country to another at a lower cost, and that kept prices down for consumers. The speed at which goods could be delivered opened America to a world of prosperity. Suddenly a wide variety of merchandise was available at affordable prices, and most folks couldn't keep their hands off of it all. The entire nation seemed to participate in a consumer feeding frenzy.

Now it may strike you as unusual, but I see in the Industrial Revolution, with its transition into a new, more aggressive capitalist economy, a wonderful model of grace. In fact, Ephesians 1 comes to mind: "[God] predestined us to be adopted as his sons through Jesus Christ...to the praise of his glorious grace, which he has freely given us in the One he loves" (verses 5–7). I believe God's grace—like the country's shift from an agriculturally based economy to an industrial one—brings to us believers a whole new level of prosperity and possibility. Through what the apostle Paul called the "surpassing grace of God in you" (2 Corinthians 9:14, NASB), our heavenly Father lifts us from where we are and transports us to the places he alone can take us. But we must stay on board even when we don't understand exactly what is happening in our lives.

Did you notice that God freely gives us his grace and that his will for each of his children is a life from which praise flows easily? God tells us in his Word that he wants to give us "beauty instead of ashes, the oil of gladness instead of mourning, and a garment of praise instead of a spirit of despair" (Isaiah 61:3). In his new economy, we don't need to stay in mourning and despair when our dreams turn to ashes. Instead we must trust in God's promise to bring beauty and gladness out of the ashes and grief; we need to leave behind the old economy and embrace the new.

Now, as we return to the life of King David, we see that he was no more immune to the old economy than we are. So far we've seen in him a person who knows what he's about, but he was also flesh and blood. In 1 Samuel 27 we see David enter a season of life where his human desires interfered with God's will. He entered into situations contradictory to the character he had modeled for so long. In short, David got off track, and watching him during this time reveals how our atmosphere can affect our attitudes and get us way off our best tracks.

## HEAVEN VERSUS HUMANITY

Tamara and I have friends who both grew up in godly homes and rarely tasted sin. At the birth of their first child, Rachel was experiencing horrendous pain, so the doctors administered epidural drugs. We went to visit her in the hospital, and she said, "Jim and Tamara, I never could figure out why young people do drugs. But I think I understand it now. It made my pain go away, and it felt so good."

In our quick-fix culture, embracing temporary fixes is incredibly tempting when we should instead deal with the deeper issues. For instance, a new job, a new relationship, or a move to a new community are, at their best, gifts from God. At their worst, however, they can be like Band-Aids applied to deeper wounds in our souls.

In 1 Samuel 27, we see David make a feel-good decision that was not in line God's will. Consequently, for sixteen months, he separated himself from God's plan, Samuel's dream, and his vision. It all started after yet another aggressive pursuit from Saul and his army. Evidently, years of pressure led David to believe that his present problems were more real than what God had promised him.

> David thought to himself, "One of these days I will be destroyed by the hand of Saul. The best thing I can do is to escape to the land of the Philistines...and I will slip out of his hand." (verse 1)

Forget the fact that David was anointed by God to be Israel's king and that he had six hundred loyal men helping him move closer every day to the fulfillment of God's purpose. David had grown pessimistic because he was tired of the pressures his problems were creating. We've all been weary—tired and tired *of.* And too often weary people disengage in the midst of difficulty. That's one way we get off track with God. We become like the Leaning Tower of Pisa in Italy: every day we get a little closer to crashing because foundational issues in our hearts need to be dealt with. And during times like these—times of stress and times of exhaustion—it's easy for us to follow our wants and lose sight of the value of obeying God.

At least it's true for me. A few times during my sixteen years as a pastor—when I've had to deal with disgruntled members, failures by staff members, and the pressures of the ministry—I've felt that it would be best to do something other than what I was doing. That's when I had to *concentrate* on God's path for me and choose to stay on track with him. I had to acknowledge that the best thing to do is always God's will, and for me that means pastoring a vibrant and life-giving church in my smaller city and helping similar churches serving throughout America's eighteen thousand smaller cities and towns.

Let's look at the steps involved in David's disengagement. First, *he embraced a negative point of view.* Notice that David thought to himself; he didn't talk with the key people God had graciously joined to his life. He didn't tell Abiathar (the man who prayed with him), he didn't bounce it off his wife, Abigail (who could have helped him manage his motivations), and he didn't tell his soldiers (who fought God's battles with him). Instead, at this point, David's feelings mattered more to him than either his faith or the counsel of those God placed in his life for fellowship.

Next, *David's negative thoughts led to negative reasoning.* David had had moments of weakness before, but this time he faced his weakness on his own, and soon everyone would suffer. David took matters into his own hands and went knocking on the door of the Philistine prince Achish. Hear David's begging: "If I have found favor in your eyes, let a place be assigned to me in one of the country towns, that I may live there. Why should your servant live in the royal city with you?" (verse 5).

Note that David was now serving the very power he had once opposed. He had run to Israel's enemy, betrayed his calling, and sworn allegiance to an ungodly king. David did not have enough faith in God to keep fighting heaven's battles, so he succumbed to the Enemy—and how many of us have been there? Sadly, we know what happens next: *negative reasoning prompts negative choices*—and those choices lead to painful circumstances God never planned for us to experience. This reasoning comes in all forms:

*It's just a little drink.*

*My parents don't want me to have any fun.*

*Everyone says he's not good for me, but...*

What starts as a personal opinion evolves into a philosophy of life:

*Church is no fun.*

*This job is getting me nowhere.*

*Marriage is a drag.*

But here is the challenge: when we fight against God's truth, we remove ourselves from the stable foundation we need in life. My friend Pat stabilized his faith, and he now enjoys a significant life as a successful pastor because he saw his problems as opportunities to prove God. David, on the other hand, learned an important lesson the hard way: *the minute our praying stops, our Enemy's preying starts.*

When we follow David's path, our whole spirits can change. We can become strangers to the dreams and visions birthed in our hearts and to the people God has brought to us.

## Responsibilities and Rewards

It is natural for our feelings to influence our choices, but we must be careful when they affect our obedience to God. And while we can't control how we feel, we must definitely control our responses to our feelings. We all want favorable circumstances, but it's not always easy to follow God's favor that leads to those circumstances. Naomi, for example, experienced this truth up close and personal. Let's shift from our friend David for a few minutes and take a look at her story in the book of Ruth.

Naomi had a husband and two sons, both of whom married outside the family faith after the four of them had left their famine-ravaged homeland to find food in Moab. First Naomi's husband died. After about ten years in Moab, she lost both of her sons, too. These days we might think of Naomi as a single mom suddenly forced to support her family. But back then, men made the living and women kept the home, so Naomi wasn't expected to support the family. That meant she was ready to ship her two daughters-in-law back to their families and their pagan gods. Essentially she said to them, "The Lord took my sons and my husband. I know that you're hurting for sure, but I'm hurting worse. So go back to where you came from. You're still young enough to start over, unlike me."

Naomi handled her pain the only way she knew how, and it's a self-directed, not a Holy Spirit–directed way. One of her daughters-in-law left, but Ruth traveled with Naomi to Bethlehem where her old friends greeted her. "Leave me alone," the old and bitter Naomi said. "The Lord doesn't love me. He has betrayed me, and I have no reason to live!"

If we've lived long enough, most of us have known such sorrow. Those of us who have lost parents know how unjust it feels. Those who have lost children know that sense of injustice even more vividly, and I am sure nobody who has not lost a child can comprehend what it feels like. Those who suffer abuse or betrayal have tasted injustice. And no matter how many suffering people we meet—and everyone suffers—we still tend to think our own wounds are greater. *Nobody knows my pain,* you think, and you're probably right. But God makes promises to people in pain, and eventually Naomi embraced that truth.

Oh, Naomi was bitter, and she had every right to be—but she still believed in God enough to recognize when he moved. So when Ruth came home one day and told Naomi about a man she'd just met, Naomi cried—as we like to say in Texas—"Lord, have mercy!" In those days the only person who could marry a widow was a relative of the widow. This man Boaz was known as a kinsman-redeemer. Related to Naomi, he could marry Ruth, and he cared enough to do so. Boaz acted in Ruth and Naomi's situation according to God's desire. He brought help and abundance to family members who were in need. That kind of unmerited favor is called grace, and Naomi recognized in Boaz what she had been seeking for many years.

That grace provision reconciled Naomi and Ruth to the purposes of God, and because of that, a faith story is born that shows the long-term reach of redemption. Ruth's marriage produced a royal family lineage—she became a great-grandmother of King David himself and therefore a distant ancestor of Jesus Christ. Neither Naomi or Ruth could have imagined such a glorious outcome when they were back in Moab grieving their losses. But they chose heaven's economy amidst their human bankruptcy and, by God's grace, were transported into an amazing place.

So hear this, my friend: you may be down, you may feel out, you might think you don't have a friend in this world or in heaven either, for that matter. But God has promised he will move if you will seek heaven's guidance amidst your heartache. Every one of us is a child of the King, and that status remains no matter what circumstances we find ourselves in or how we got there.

Returning to David, let's examine him as a son in need of God's grace. When I think of his wandering at this point, I think of getting back a report card or test. Do you remember bringing home tests you'd taken in school? You could, for instance, have gotten forty-six of the fifty questions on the math test right, but still your eyes went straight to those four red marks. It didn't matter that the teacher wrote "Excellent!" on the top of your paper or if she put two star stickers in the corner. That's because our shortcomings bother us. They're too real a reminder that we aren't perfect, and we fear falling short of human expectations. We have all felt like David when he said, "Man, this is hard work. I might as well quit now because I'll fail someday anyway" (1 Samuel 27:1, my paraphrase). Compromise seldom happens overnight; rather it grows in our hearts, and we usually act upon it whenever our human feelings overpower our faith in heaven's plan. We see that David compromised in two distinct ways.

First, *David ignored God's purposes and pursued pleasure instead.* David lived in enemy territory for a year and four months, the Bible reports. While he may have enjoyed the *presents* of man, he was ignoring the *presence* of God. Scholars say that none of David's more than one hundred psalms were penned during these sixteen months.

Next, *David built wrong partnerships with people who affirmed his errant ways.* He closed his ears to godly companions and opened them to pagan influence.

Having strayed from God, David turned into a savage: "Whenever David attacked an area, he did not leave a man or woman alive, but took sheep and cattle, donkeys and camels, and clothes" (1 Samuel 27:9).

David also turned into a liar. When Prince Achish asked him, "Where did you go raiding today?" David never informed the barbarian king of his exact whereabouts. That's one reason why he killed every person in the villages he ravaged: "They might inform on us and say, 'This is what David did'" (verses 10–11).

David felt really smart; he'd pulled one over on the king. And isn't that exactly how we feel when we live on a side track? We first submit to temptation, and then we lie to save face or protect ourselves. We partake of forbidden pleasure and then pretend we're innocent. Illicit pleasure is fun—and the more we experience it, the more addictive it becomes. It also causes us to enter places where we don't belong, but we go there anyway because belonging somewhere is better than being alone.

Early in his life, David used his energy to pursue God's will, but now his days were his alone. He no longer prayed for God's will, and he no longer lived for God's praise. He denied the character that had made him a great leader, he forsook the Spirit of God, and he silenced his godly partners. Even King Achish saw how sidetracked David was, saying to himself, "He has become so odious to his people, the Israelites, that he will be my servant forever" (1 Samuel 27:12).

It's interesting to watch where David went from this point. David soon realized that losing his concentration was costly. *Circumstances eventually reveal that it doesn't pay for us to pursue success at the expense of our significance.* The orchestrations of life's events teach all of us that lesson sooner or later, don't they? And when they do, the Holy Spirit's presence assures us that blessed days can lie ahead if we are ready to handle the responsibility that comes with living a life of significance.

# CHAPTER 8

## Our Loco-Motives

Any of you who speak Spanish—or who watch Speedy Gonzales—know the word *loco*. It means "crazy," and since we just discussed the steam-driven locomotive as a symbol for changing to a divine economy, talking now about *loco*-motives seems logical. A motive is defined in Webster's dictionary as "something that causes a person to act," and we all know that acting the right way is not always easy. We want to do what is holy and God-honoring, but when our emotions and human desires go unmet, the temptation is great to put self ahead of God.

Let me share a story about Shelly, one of the few Christians in my high school. At the time, only a handful of kids were living for God, and we all huddled together in fellowship to survive.

Well, all the guys in our group thought we would be holier if we didn't date. (Looking back now, I think we replaced sin with stupidity.) Well, Shelly was social and missed the intimacy that dating relationships offered her. She also thought the school needed more Christians, so she started in on a campaign to date non-Christian guys and lead them to the Lord. All the Christian guys freaked out, but she stepped out anyway. I'll tell you, I thought it then and I think it now: my daughters will never date the kind of guys Shelly brought around.

One night we all saw Shelly at a dance with a guy who definitely had a terrible case of Saturday night fever. When we saw her on Monday, Shelly was not quite herself, and we asked her what had happened. She explained that the guy had made a move on her in the car on the way home. She stopped him and started telling him about Jesus, and the guy said something all girls should hear: "If you're one of those Christians, what are you doing hanging out here? People like that shouldn't be with guys like me."

In the church, we call Shelly's desire missionary dating, and it often happens when young Christians are not ready to fully commit themselves to holiness, so they excuse their passions and desires by making their intentions sound God-honoring. Their intentions don't honor God, though, and we can all think of people who are in sad circumstances today that have their roots in some crazy choices. I'm glad Shelly eventually settled in with a great guy for the long haul, but for many people, stability never comes. Instead the church becomes a distant memory, and when people ask them if they go to church, they answer, "Church is nothing but a bunch of hypocrites"—as if the bar scene is filled with people of integrity.

People who act crazy, succumbing to those *loco*-motives and trying to defend wrong actions as right, make enemies out of those who should be friends. When people have *loco*-motives, they distance themselves from helpful relationships and lie about harmful relationships they enter into. Crazy people ignore the truth, rephrasing it in a way that justifies their pur-

suit of wrong pleasures. And attempting to believe that spin—when everyone around you knows better—is crazy too.

Also, keep in mind that our sinful world stands ready to receive any of
God's fallen saints. The more who join a hellish lifestyle, the more justified
the others feel. In fact, the sinful world smiles when God's people compromise their holiness; it makes the world's redefinition of *right* more
acceptable. *After all, because of what I've been through, don't I have the right
to do what I feel like doing?* The excessive booze, the parties, the impure
relationships—*Why not, if it makes me feel better today?*

I've heard that argument many times, and here is my answer: Do you
think your choices will one day actually produce the circumstances you
desire? I have seen so many cave in and suffer the painful circumstances
that compromise produces. I know *it takes power to lead a holy life,
but the rewards far outweigh the requirements.*

In the case of David, there is a scripture that deserves a closer look. In
1 Samuel 16, we read that when Samuel anointed David as king, he poured
oil on the young man's head. The oil soaked in to David's skin as a reminder
of God's abiding presence with him:

> So Samuel took the horn of oil and anointed him in the
> presence of his brothers, and from that day on the Spirit
> of the LORD came upon David in power. (verse 13)

The Holy Spirit gave David the power he needed to prevail over
Goliath. The Spirit gave David the power to rout the Philistine army and
resist the continual assaults of Saul and his army. But David temporarily
lost the battle against his greatest enemy of all—his sinful nature. How
many of us can say the same? *Why do we cave in instead of craving God's
help?*

## CAVED-IN CONFIDENCE

Remember my friend Pat Butcher and his drowned pigs? I'd like to share a story about his wife at this point because it will help us learn to do a better job handling life's pressures. Pat is married to a wonderful and godly woman named Brooke. Now Brooke was not faithful to church as a child, so her choices were often more feelings-motivated than faith-motivated. But in her late twenties Brooke surrendered her life to God, and soon afterward she received a spiritual mother who taught her what the life of faith was all about. Brooke's spiritual mother happened to be Pat Butcher's aunt, and everybody knows that mothers and aunts in the South feel called to find each of their sons and nephews a good woman to marry.

Brooke didn't exactly have a man like Pat in mind, but after failing to pick out good men when she acted on her feelings, she was done making her own decisions. She remembers having it out with God one day when she was feeling lonely. Finally she said, "I want you to pick the man, Lord." Their story wasn't immediately a happily-ever-after one, though, because when they first were to meet, Brooke explains, "Pat wouldn't even come out of his room." But eventually he did, and the two married shortly thereafter.

When Brooke moved from a big city to Pat's small town, the transition was not easy. Pat was a pastor, and that made her a pastor's wife—and aren't pastors' wives supposed to be perfect? "I tried to live according to everyone's expectations," Brooke said, "but I got pressed in by what the congregation wanted me to be."

I find this story interesting because Pat and Brooke, two very different individuals, were fighting the same battle against pressure. Pat was trying to plant a significant church in a small town, and Brooke was trying to be the perfect pastor's wife—and they both felt the kind of pressure that can drive us crazy. And pressure builds when problems seem more real to us than God's promises, doesn't it? Pressure gives birth to pessimism. That's why a wise older pastor cautioned me "to pursue God more than my goals because human desires can breed frustration whereas living by faith always breeds confidence."

That's a lesson David had learned earlier but somehow forgotten. He knew the Holy Spirit's presence. He had felt the Spirit's power as the warmth of that anointing oil dripped down his face, over his shoulder, along his spine, right down to his feet. However, when the pressures of life grew greater than he'd ever expected, David acted according to how he felt instead of following the One he had been anointed to serve.

Think back to the idea David first entertained and then later embraced: "One of these days I will be destroyed by the hand of Saul. The best thing I can do is to escape to the land of the Philistines. Then Saul will give up searching for me anywhere in Israel, and I will slip out of his hand" (1 Samuel 27:1). David was right. Running from God's call allowed him to escape the pressure of Saul's pursuit, but it also separated him from God's presence and power. Not only did David lose his joy and sense of fulfillment during that time, but his choice eventually led to circumstances that brought him even greater pressure. Isn't that what happens when we cave in instead of craving God's help?

Back to David's story. With David in his corner, the Philistine king aggressively acted on his passionate hatred of Israel:

> In those days the Philistines gathered their forces to fight
> against Israel. Achish said to David, "You must understand
> that you and your men will accompany me in the army.

David said, "Then you will see for yourself what your servant can do." (1 Samuel 28:1–2)

To better appreciate this arrangement, imagine Palestine's Hamas Party enlisting Israel's best general to attack his native country. It's impossible! It's ridiculous! No sane person would believe it. Israel is so dear to those who understand God's purpose for their country that they could never fight for its destruction.

But that's what happens when we two-time God: *David conducted himself like those who needed to be converted* and found himself fighting against what he knew he should be fighting for. David's lack of confidence in God's ability to deliver him from Saul had prompted him to take a wrong path.

And are you all that different from David? Are you confident in God's ability to deliver you from the Sauls in your life? Know that God wants to bring pleasure, he wants your Christian home to be beautiful and comfortable, he wants your career to satisfy the desires of your heart, and he wants to fulfill his promises to you. But you must learn to deal with the pressure. God says essentially, "I've shown you my will. Now please let me work—and remember that my purposes for your life don't change just because some places you find yourself along the way seem unpleasant."

Have you, though, ever been in the midst of a downward spiral and asked yourself where it all began? Most of the time, caved-in confidence amidst pressure has motivated crazy decisions that brought forth painful consequences.

During those times we must remind ourselves, like Naomi, to persevere through pain. We also must remember that—as Pat and Brooke Butcher experienced—our plans won't always seem to be working out, but

God's plan always will. It is so easy to get cynical when difficulties threaten our dreams, but wise people remember that our circumstances will eventually reflect God's grace if we make the right choices.

We must always remember that God promises grace amidst our grief. He says:

> He will call upon me, and I will answer him;
>> I will be with him in trouble,
>> I will deliver him and honor him.
> With long life will I satisfy him
>> and show him my salvation. (Psalm 91:15–16)

God knows what our futures hold. He knows every trap the Enemy has waiting for us—and he promises to free us from them all.

Craving God's presence turned David from a neglected son into a national hero. Caved-in confidence led him into problems he couldn't solve on his own. And, incidentally, that same inability to manage selfish motives eventually cost Saul his position as king.

## CAVED-IN COURAGE

I love baseball, and because of that I'm full of stories about the greatest men who ever played the game. I love the story about Mickey Mantle when he first broke into the major leagues.

Mickey came from Commerce, Oklahoma, where his father refined his incredible, raw athletic talent. Despite that talent, during Mickey's first year in the majors, he struggled to hit the ball, and he was booed so badly that the Yankees sent him back to Triple-A (the minor leagues) in Kansas City. The game that had once come so easily for Mickey now seemed more like work. Never before had he had to work hard for success, and the pressure was eroding his confidence.

One night, in a fit of frustration, Mickey called home and told his dad that he was through with baseball. His dad got in the car that minute and drove several hours to Mickey's hotel room. Now before you rush to any conclusions, you need to know that life had been difficult for Mr. Mantle. He had worked in the mines his whole life and raised his family during one of the darkest economic periods America has ever known. Mr. Mantle had hoped to escape the Dust Bowl years earlier by getting his own contract to play professional ball, but when it didn't come, he turned his attention to his son Mickey.

What's more, Mr. Mantle was dying of cancer, so he had little sympathy for his boy who was betraying the family dream. When Mickey, who thought his father was coming to encourage him, opened the hotel-room door, Mr. Mantle blew right past him, grabbed a suitcase, and started packing his son's bags.

"What're you doing?" Mickey complained.

"Taking you home," his father said.

"Why?"

His father turned to him, crying. "I thought I raised a man… You ain't nothin' but a coward."

That moment, Mickey Mantle said, changed his life forever. In those seconds he realized that refusing to face his problems meant forsaking a dream that held the power to bless those he loved.

Both Saul and David were forsaking dreams that held the power to bless those they loved. At the time neither of them understood the grave consequences of their actions because they focused on themselves instead of on their faith-calling. This is one reason why God eventually removed Saul as king. Simply put, Saul adopted a lifestyle when he *put his own motives ahead of God's.* By contrast, God's Word removes all doubt about folly of doing so:

> After removing Saul, [God] made David their king. [God] testified concerning him: "I have found David son of Jesse a man after my own heart; he will do everything I want him to do." (Acts 13:22)

God's people follow God's heart and make his purposes their priority. People seldom see their hopes come crashing down overnight. Rather, as I mentioned earlier, like the Leaning Tower of Pisa, we creep closer to our destruction inch by inch. Sensing ourselves caving in is a sure sign that we have deep heart issues that need correction. Saul's heart had drifted away from God over a decade earlier, and now his insecurity got the best of him.

In 1 Samuel 28, when Saul saw the Philistines approaching, "he was afraid; terror filled his heart" (verse 5). Saul had lost the power of the Holy Spirit, the mentor who had once guided him (Samuel), and his best servant (David). We see sin slowly having its way in Saul's life: first sin deceives us, then it draws us away from God's presence, and then destruction overcomes us.

In the face of the Philistine army, Saul "inquired of the LORD, but the LORD did not answer him" (verse 6). He knew this might be the end, and in desperation he commanded his attendants to find him a witch. He wanted somebody—anybody—who could tell him what was about to happen. Not giving up on Saul, God tried to turn him from sin by telling him through a witch that he and his sons would die if they engaged the Philistines in battle (see verses 8–20).

When Saul "inquired of the LORD," he hoped to change his circumstances instantly, but they had been sealed long ago by his crazy actions. I can't help but feel sorry for Saul, for it is clear he had moments of sanity. In 1 Samuel 24, for instance, and not long before his death, Saul acknowledged God's plan. Speaking to David, he said, "I know that you will surely be king and that the kingdom of Israel will be established in your hands" (verse 20). Even closer to the time of his death and the death of his sons, he made a promise to David, who had spared the king's life a second time: "Because you considered my life precious today, I will not try to harm you again.... May you be blessed, my son David; you will do great things and surely triumph" (1 Samuel 26:21, 25).

But why did David recover from his poor choices and Saul die because of his? Because David eventually recognized his immaturity while Saul insisted on having his own way to the end. He never realized that his deficient character would undo any worthy dreams that he had. *Saul's outcome was a result of his convictions.*

## CRAVING GOD'S HELP

*Loco*-motives. We've probably all acted on them at one time or another. And we probably all know that sorting out our motives isn't a job for cowards. Yet God promises to strengthen us in our struggles, and he gives us the right to make choices. Romans 3:23 says, "All have sinned and fall short of the glory of God." What will you choose to do after you sin? Will you let the effects of that failure be only momentary, or will you choose failure as a way of life?

Ultimately, Saul failed because he continually put his will ahead of God's. David, on the other hand, exited failure because he learned his lesson and put God's will ahead of his own.

It's all too easy, though, to give in to what God forbids because of how we feel. We are all tempted to pursue more-pleasurable options when our obedience to God brings us pressure. That's why many of us may fall onto side tracks. *Pressure and adversity form a large part of life, but be encouraged that a significant life still awaits those who, like David and my friends Pat and Brooke, figure out that obedience doesn't really cost; it pays.* When we concentrate on God's will in the midst of life's madness, we avoid the temptation to get on board our own *loco*-motive and jump the tracks.

# CHAPTER 9

## Full Steam Ahead

A re you one of those people wanting to get back on God's track? If so, I want to encourage you that a significant life awaits. You haven't missed out—though I haven't always been so sure of that truth. Early in my Christian life, I thought my human imperfections were more than capable of sabotaging God's plans. But since that time, years of studying the Bible and helping lots of people have convinced me that God always has a way to bless a willing heart!

Let me illustrate that good news by once more using the railroad. As I mentioned earlier, the transcontinental railroad, completed in 1869, changed the nation's way of life. Railroads lowered the cost of shipping and shortened the time that products were in transit, so soon everyone realized that a more prosperous economy was possible *for some.*

Certain parts of our nation, however, had a much more difficult time getting on board the railroad revolution. It was fairly easy, for instance, to lay the railroad track across the plains and to build the steam engines capable of traveling that level land. But what about the Rocky Mountains? The prosperity enabled by the railroad system didn't include everybody immediately.

But the people of the great Northwest had a strong desire to be part of the railroad system, a desire that wouldn't be denied. So railroad track was eventually laid from Sherman Hills, Wyoming, through the rugged Rocky Mountains, and into Utah. From there, they could ship goods by stagecoach wherever they needed to go.

To travel that stretch of railroad, the largest steam engine in the world had to be designed and built, the Union Pacific No. 4017. It was named Big Boy, and the name was quite appropriate because no other train could carry the heavy freight across the rugged Rockies.

God created all of us to be Big Boys and Big Girls—to bear our heavy burdens across the rugged terrain of life. Isn't that what Paul taught the Corinthians? He said:

> No test or temptation that comes your way is beyond
> the course of what others have had to face. All you need
> to remember is that God will never let you down; he'll
> never let you be pushed past your limit; he'll always be
> there to help you come through it. (1 Corinthians
> 10:13, MSG)

Haven't we all been there, feeling like we can't possibly go on, thinking that this challenge is beyond our abilities? Haven't we all asked, "God, can

I quit now?" Yes, we've all been there, but the answer to that question about quitting is no because God always has enough grace to transport you to your next place of blessing. *Your course is not too difficult because God is traveling with you. He will never let you down, and he will never push you past your limit.* Instead, he will always be there to help you through whatever challenges you face. So develop a lifestyle of trust in God, and soon the temptation to quit when difficulties arise will lose its grip in your life. And you will experience prizes worth their price.

Let me bring the story of Pat and Brooke to a close. What was the starting point for Pat's incredible life of service? Pat says he told God, "I wouldn't choose me. I'd rather be in the fields with hogs than up here with people. Besides, I'm a single guy without a ministry partner."

Where are Pat and Brooke today? His church has grown. Now four hundred fifty of the ten thousand people in his county are active members of his church. That is 4.5 percent of his county population—not huge by big-city standards—but let me put the numbers in perspective. If a church in a city of one million people reached 4.5 percent of the population, forty-five thousand people would be attending weekend services. *Pat is now helping a higher percentage of the people living near his church than almost any pastor in America.*

In addition, he has a pretty incredible ministry partner in Brooke. And he better remember it wasn't just his farm-boy good looks that attracted her. She was looking for a man of God to enjoy her life with.

Recently I was with Pat and Brooke for their third annual old-fashioned picnic. What a sight! In that county of ten thousand people, thirty-six hundred people showed up to enjoy tractor-pull competitions, an antique car show, horse racing, horseshoes, and more games and food than anyone could indulge in! It was the South at its best—forty churches joined together to let the community know that God and his church are intent on bringing life to the community around them.

Pat has a hard time explaining *how* all this happened. He just knows that they rented the local fairgrounds for the event, and soon people from everywhere brought tractors, cars, horses, horseshoes, games, and food. Pat has no problem at all, however, explaining *why* all this happened: "The psalms say that our help comes from the sanctuary and Zion. Zion is the leadership that gives direction, and the sanctuary is where God dwells among his people. You have to find what stretches faith in you. Do that and God will bring people alongside to help."

Back now to David and his preparations for an amazing journey out of destruction and discouragement and toward fulfilled dreams. David and his men will show us how to follow God's sometimes-difficult track to restoration and blessing.

## GAINING STEAM

David was to be king sooner than he thought and sooner than anyone else imagined—but first he faced a mountain range of difficulties resulting from his wrong motives and deeds.

In 1 Samuel 29, David discovered that people who play with fire get burned. Prompted by Philistine commanders who feared David would turn against them as they fought Israel, Prince Achish dismissed him from the Philistine army. They argued, "How better could he regain his master's favor than by taking the heads of our own men?" (verse 4). Prince Achish had found David reliable and without fault, but he couldn't defy the commanders who disapproved of David.

So, dismissed from the Philistine army, David and his men head back to their town, Ziklag, while the Philistines fight Saul and his army in Jezreel:

> David and his men reached Ziklag on the third day. Now the Amalekites had raided the Negev and Ziklag. They had attacked Ziklag and burned it, and had taken captive the women and all who were in it, both young and old. They killed none of them, but carried them off as they went on their way.
>
> When David and his men came to Ziklag, they found it destroyed by fire and their wives and sons and daughters taken captive. (1 Samuel 30:1–3)

David and his men wept aloud, the Bible says, "until they had no strength left to weep" (verse 4). But then David faced a greater challenge than grief: his men spoke of stoning him because, in their minds, he was the reason for their grief. *Why did we follow him in the first place? I should have listened to my wife. She told me to leave this army months ago!* I'm sure thoughts like these were in the men's minds.

But David immediately did something that reminded everybody why they had followed him originally. David turned to God. He knew that God was the only One who could put enough steam in everybody's engine to cross those mountains of difficulty.

Where else could David have turned? His family was gone, and his friends no longer trusted him. But David understood what the apostle Paul said we will all need to learn eventually—to pass through our difficulties into our destinies, we must believe our courses are never beyond God's ability or power.

Think of the famous freedom fighter Nelson Mandela, who spent decades of his life fighting racial oppression in South Africa. He was harassed, put on trial, and forced underground when his political activity was suppressed by gunfire. His first wife left him, and I'm sure his children often wondered if the cost of their father's cause was worth it.

Yet today Mr. Mandela is enthroned in the hearts of black South Africans as the father of their freedom, the representative of fairness and justice, the hero of a people who have learned what great blessings lie on the other side of difficult battles.

But why was Mr. Mandela able to prevail through decades of difficulty? I'm convinced that he persevered because he believed his cause was just. He also believed he had the strength necessary to sustain him through every single difficulty that would threaten the dream. I recently watched a documentary about his life, and I wept as I beheld the people's love for this man who epitomized their dream. When he was forced underground, they sacrificially provided for him because of their devotion to the dream. When he was imprisoned, they risked their lives when they joined together outside the prison grounds and loudly chanted, "Free Nelson Mandela."

No doubt Mr. Mandela possessed extraordinary leadership skills. But they alone weren't enough. He also had the personal survival skills of belief, tenacity, and perseverance.

In addition, he had to inspire a great team to fight sacrificially for the cause. In his biography, he speaks of his second wife, Winnie, coming to see him in prison: "I told her to tell the children of my capture.... I said we were not the first family in this situation, those who underwent such hardship came out the stronger." Then he said, "I assured her of the strength of our cause...and [reminded her] how it would be her love and devotion that would see me through whatever transpired." The apartheid government of South Africa eventually had to recognize the truth that the African National Congress was no mealy-mouthed youth movement; it was comprised of people strong enough to seize their freedom.

In a similar way, David became a source of strength for his men when they needed it most. The Bible says, "But David found strength in the LORD his God" (1 Samuel 30:6). He called his old friend and priest Abiathar, and David again asked for the ephod, symbolizing his belief that God's Spirit would show the way to overcome every difficulty that threatened his destiny. David didn't live weighed down with regrets about the past; he lived with an eye for the future and sought the reward God promises to all who believe in heaven's purposes amidst personal failure. David then did four things that enabled God to transport him to his next place of blessing.

## PRAY AND OBEY

Prayer is the first step to take when you want enough steam in your engine to enable success. Over the years, I have had the privilege of seeing numerous spouses reconcile with each other and enjoy rich and rewarding marriages. I have seen people of all ages reinvigorated by God's dreams for them, and I've rejoiced as God provided what was necessary for them to turn those dreams into reality.

Such God-glorifying success stories begin with a belief in what he promises—and David had that kind of faith:

> David inquired of the LORD, "Shall I pursue this raiding
> party? Will I overtake them?"

"Pursue them,' [God] answered. "You will certainly over-take them and succeed in the rescue." (1 Samuel 30:8)

Regrets or rewards—which do you see ahead of you after you fail? Your answer may depend on whether you are trained in the art of prayer. I've learned that praying people can trust God to keep his dreams alive in their hearts.

One day when I was praying, the Lord impressed on me a truth that helps me especially when I fight battles initiated by my own failures. I realized that everything God ever promised to do in my life, he promised knowing every mistake I'd ever make.

The Bible teaches that God is *omniscient.* The word *omniscient* means he has "infinite understanding." He knows all that was, and is, and ever will be. The Bible teaches that God is *omnipotent. Omnipotent* means that he has "infinite power" at his disposal. Finally, the book of Ephesians says, "In him we were also chosen, having been predestined according to the plan of him who works out everything in conformity with the purpose of his will" (1:11).

It is easy to believe in and continually pursue my destiny once I understand an omniscient, omnipotent God has given me a "predestiny." The word *predestined* means "determined beforehand." God determined before he ever gave us his dreams for our lives that he would be all we need to overcome the obstacles.

## PURSUE GOD'S PROMISES

After he prayed, David's obedience added more steam to the engine. Trusting God to be faithful, he followed the Lord's instructions and marched into battle:

David and the six hundred men with him came to the Besor Ravine, where some stayed behind, for two hundred men were too exhausted to cross the ravine. But David and four hundred men continued the pursuit.

They found an Egyptian in a field and…gave him water to drink. (1 Samuel 30:9–11)

Do you see how the spirit of David's men began to change? David's men, who so quickly turned savage in the Philistines' land, now extended grace to the Egyptian: "They gave him water to drink and food to eat—part of a cake of pressed figs and two cakes of raisins. He ate and was revived, for he had not eaten any food or drunk any water for three days and three nights" (verses 11–12).

When David asked the Egyptian, "To whom do you belong, and where do you come from?" (verse 13), the man explained that he was a servant of the people who had raided David's village. He also offered to lead David to where the raiding party was. Take note: only moments earlier all the men were separated from their families and their possessions, and the men spoke seriously of stoning David. Now the Egyptian promised to take them to the Amalekite camp where their families and possessions were.

*That's what prayer can do, but its power is only experienced by people who believe in it enough to pursue what God has promised.* What would have happened if David and all six hundred of his men had stopped on the far side of the Besor Ravine due to exhaustion? The Egyptian in the desert would have died from starvation. David's army would have missed the restoration of their families and possessions even though God had provided for it. Grab on to that important truth: God's dream for us will require our participation even when it isn't easy. That's why we must resist the temptation to stop when we're tired. I wonder how many Christians have missed God's blessing because they quit when they were exhausted instead of continuing in their pursuit of God's purpose.

## PASSIONATELY ACT

Have you ever wondered why our dreams require so much of us? I have. Many of God's blessings that I enjoy today demanded sacrificial effort not easy for me to put forth. That's one reason why grace can be so hard to understand: it's free, yet it demands our all.

David experienced grace, but it required great effort on his part:

> [The Egyptian] led David down, and there they were, scattered over the countryside, eating, drinking and reveling because of the great amount of plunder they had taken.... David fought them from dusk until the evening of the next day, and none of them got away, except four hundred young men who rode off on camels and fled. David recovered everything the Amalekites had taken. (1 Samuel 30:16–18)

Every wife, every child, and the plunder—all was recovered. But that recovery required David to fight from dusk one day until the evening of the next day. How did he do it? I believe he was able to because when you're acting on your passions, they energize you. When you are living for the reasons God placed you upon this earth, putting forth even monumental effort fulfills you far more than taking it easy does. Somehow you know that, with every step you take, you are moving closer to the reward your heart seeks.

Another example comes to mind. Recently I was incredibly blessed by the testimony of a man who attended our church before he moved to San Antonio. We've never met, but the church he now attends in San Antonio publishes stories about God's work in their members' lives. Because our church was instrumental in his story, someone sent a copy to me.

This man lost his entire family in the mid-1990s. He was playing basketball three or four nights a week, and if he didn't do that, he went drinking with his buddies after work. After a couple of years of that behavior, his marriage was understandably strained.

He said he was also taking steroids at the time to get stronger, and they made him angry: "I was cussing like a sailor all the time." He was spending money foolishly, and his wife couldn't keep them out of debt even though she worked full-time and cared for their small children. Eventually she had enough.

The breaking point came when they lost their home. His wife said, "We are in debt. I can't pay for our home. I can't raise our children myself. I'm going out on my own."

When his wife came with a U-Haul to move her things out, he remembers looking in the mirrors of the truck as she drove away and watching tears stream down her cheeks and the cheeks of his children. He thought, *Look what my wrong lifestyle has cost everybody.*

His employer transferred him to Victoria from San Antonio. He wasn't a committed believer at the time, but he knew he needed God's help so he enrolled in a one-year Bible correspondence program. Then he heard of our new nondenominational church just built, and he thought, "Man, I need to go there."

He came and gave his life to the Lord—and he kept coming week after week. When his wife brought the children to Victoria to see him, she noticed the huge change in him. To make a long story short, the family is now reconciled, they have recovered it all, and they are leaders in their local church helping restore others. When we act passionately toward fulfilling God's purposes, our lives are transformed.

## PRACTICE MERCY

David realized that his poor choices had negatively affected a lot of people. I'm sure he regretted all he had put his men and their families through. On the way back to Ziklag with his men, their families, and their plunder, he reunited with the two hundred men who had quit due to exhaustion:

> They came out to meet David and the people with him. As David and his men approached, he greeted them. But all the evil men and troublemakers among David's followers said, "Because they did not go out with us, we will not share with them the plunder we recovered. However, each man may take his wife and children and go." (1 Samuel 30:21–22)

David's response to the troublemakers' proposal was simple and straightforward: no. The share of the plunder given to the men who stayed behind with the supplies was to be the same as that of the men who went to battle. "All will share alike," David commanded in verse 24. In addition, "He sent some of the plunder to the elders of Judah, who were his friends, saying, 'Here is a present for you from the plunder of the LORD's enemies'" (verse 26).

David knew what he was doing. He had seen firsthand how focusing on oneself had disastrous consequences, and he was ready to make choices that benefited God, himself, and others.

## FULL STEAM AHEAD

Pray and obey. Pursue God's promises. Passionately act. Practice mercy. When David did these things, God moved him along the path toward blessing. Yet, needless to say, many things can derail our prayers, actions, and mercy. In fact, there are many ways we can stop short of living significant lives. Our weaknesses tempt us to settle for less, and they try to convince us that our *confidence* in God won't make a difference in our circumstances. A world opposed to God's will also challenges our godly pursuits, and only persevering *character* provides the power to overcome. And pressure will constantly tempt us to take an easier road, and that's when we must remind ourselves to *concentrate* on doing God's will. *Obedience brings rewards, not regrets; obedience is the path to the next place of God's grace.*

Now back to David. He had been home in Ziklag for just a couple days when a messenger brought him the news that Saul was dead. The messenger also brought the crown that had been on Saul's head (see 2 Samuel 1:4, 10).

At this crucial turning point in David's life when he's finally about to wear the crown promised to him years earlier, let's ask ourselves why David finally became king. Was it because his kingship was God's dream? Yes. Was it because of David's obedience? Yes. But the truth is God needed David and the people as partners to prevail, and David also needed God and the people as partners to prevail. Just like Nelson Mandela and Pat and Brooke needed lots of people concentrating on doing right together to produce a greater future.

Our help does come from the sanctuary and from Zion. So let God guide you into what stretches your faith. Watch him bring good people alongside you to help—people who understand and draw from the divine power necessary for living life on purpose and with passion. As we keep these truths in mind—as we concentrate on obeying God's will alongside the team members he gives us—we'll discover a satisfaction and contentment that difficult circumstances can't take away. Your significant life is now full steam ahead!

# PART IV

# Cooperation

*Blessed are those you choose*
*and bring near to live in your courts!*
*We are filled with the good things of your house,*
*of your holy temple.*

PSALM 65:4

# CHAPTER 10

*Tug of War*

William Carey was an eighteenth-century English pastor working as a cobbler to make ends meet when he sensed God's calling to take the gospel to India. Though the British colonials viewed India's populace as heathen, Carey knew that the redemptive power of God's grace would provide what was necessary to break inhumane bondage and bring countless blessings. As he prepared to resign from his small country church, Carey found many cynics and few supporters. Even his spiritual advisors thought he was crazy and made statements like "God can reach the heathen without your help whenever he is ready to do so." Carey knew that God did not *have* to use him, but he felt strongly that God *wanted* to use him.

Even Carey's wife didn't want him to go, but his conviction was so great that he determined to go alone if she stayed behind. Finally, compelled by her husband's resolve, Dorothy Carey relented, and she and their four children moved to India with William. The weeks in Calcutta turned into months, and the missionary funds provided by his home church were soon gone. Yet Carey maintained his dream of converting natives of India to his life-giving faith. He started cobbling shoes again, planted a garden, and began rebuilding his life in an unfamiliar culture. He and his family endured unsanitary living conditions, dysentery, near starvation, and ravaging fevers, one of which left Carey bald for the rest of his life.

William Carey spent over forty years, more than half his life, in India as a preacher, translator, shoemaker, botanist, and social reformer. However, he led only a handful of people to the Lord. Most people today—with a bigger-is-always-better bias—would view his mission as unsuccessful. And if Carey's peers had considered only numbers, his life would have been unimpressive at best and maybe even ignored. But William Carey's impact on India and the world continues today: God turned that first handful of believers into a bucketful. Later that bucketful became more bucketfuls and then bushels, and today *fifty million* people in India call Jesus their Lord and Savior, and *hundreds of millions* of people around the world are Christians because of the modern missionary movement sparked by William Carey.

If Carey had listened to the cynics back home, including his wife, he would not have become the father of modern missions. He proved by example that reaching the heathen is possible for those willing to endure much suffering and hardship. And we can be encouraged by Carey's example. After all, your significant life and mine will probably require at least one seemingly unfruitful season when we feel as though we're spinning our wheels, as if our efforts are yielding little return. *Living significant lives requires us to cooperate with God when cynics say our efforts aren't worth it.*

## Push and Pull

Resilient obedience is what William Carey demonstrated, and it's required of all of us before we receive life's greatest rewards. Our relationships with God will involve give and take, and people who aren't convinced that God's reward is coming will eventually lose the resolve necessary to continue cooperating with his plan. When something disappointing happens, these people act rashly instead of obeying God and waiting on him. When they don't get what they want right away, they are filled with negativity instead of staying filled with hope. When people discourage or disapprove of them, they seek something pleasurable instead of seeking the approval of God.

William Carey had every opportunity to be one of these people and die a sad and unfulfilled man. Yes, he heard God's call, he felt God's touch, and he was compelled to act, but he also faced hurdle after hurdle and extreme difficulties. Human beings provided lots of interference, but despite all the pain and hardship, Carey was determined to keep cooperating with God.

How about you? We all have some sense of the groups of people and the situations we'd like to be a part of someday—if everyone cooperated! But what are we willing to settle for today amidst human failures? Or what do we settle for after our dream worlds crumble because somebody violated our trust? As time goes on, cynical voices within and without tell us that our dreams aren't worth the effort.

Think about the dreams you had as a kid. Some of us wanted to be professional athletes, fly to the moon, or be successful women with happy families. Difficult circumstances can prompt us to dismiss our dreams, can't they? Voices of opposition—"Who are you kidding?" and "As if you could ever do that!"—can discourage us. Afraid that a child might end up disappointed, a parent might try to refocus him or her: "Instead of flying to the moon as an astronaut, why don't you just fly airplanes?" A discouraged friend, speaking from personal experience, might say, "Forget about marriage. All the good ones are taken anyway." Like being in a tug of war, pursuing a dream can be hard.

Yet, like William Carey, David has proved by example that God greatly rewards resilient obedience. His cooperation with God moved him forward from poor shepherd boy to prominent military leader to courageous cave man to king. In 2 Samuel 2, David addressed the men of Jabesh Gilead following his coronation as king of Judah: "Now then, be strong and brave, for Saul your master is dead, and the house of Judah has anointed me over them" (verse 7).

David spoke these words after the valiant men of Jabesh Gilead had just buried Saul and his sons. Earlier the Philistines had cut off Saul's head and fastened his dead body—along with the bodies of his sons—to the wall of Beth Shan in their territory (see 1 Samuel 31:8–10). It was one way they celebrated their victory over the Israelites.

But those men of Jabesh Gilead journeyed through the night to Beth Shan, took the bodies of Saul and his sons down from the wall, and carried them back to Israel for a proper burial (see verses 11–13). Second Samuel 1 closes with David's lament for Saul and Jonathan, a song he ordered all the men of Judah to learn. Calling Saul and Jonathan "the glory" of Israel, David expressed gratitude for their accomplishments, for the prosperity they had brought Israel, and for the positive things done for him personally, especially by Jonathan.

To me, that lament gives us a pretty vivid picture of why David kept moving toward an even more significant life. The Bible promises in Romans 8:28, "In all things God works for the good of those who love him, who have been called according to his purpose." Yet it is so easy when things aren't going our way to love God more casually and to abandon his purposes to pursue our own.

Life is full of tugs of war, and one reason why people end up rewarded is they consistently stay on the right side during the struggle. God doesn't promise the elimination of skirmishes, but he promises to be with us. As soon as David encouraged the men of Jabesh Gilead to be strong and brave, he entered into the next skirmish.

## GOD'S WILL VERSUS OTHER PEOPLE'S WILLS

David learned in 2 Samuel 2 that the majority of Israel's leaders were still not on board with him. Saul had one son who was still alive, Ish-Bosheth, and the leaders of Israel made him their king despite the fact that the tribe of Judah had already made David king.

> Abner son of Ner, the commander of Saul's army, had taken
> Ish-Bosheth son of Saul and brought him over to Mahanaim.
> He made him king over Gilead, Ashuri and Jezreel, and also
> over Ephraim, Benjamin and all Israel. (verses 8–9)

What a disappointment! Remember the expectation in David's words when he spoke to the men of Jabesh Gilead? He thought he would soon be king and better times would prevail, but that expectation was quickly denied. Other people's wishes were not lining up with the will of God. In my father's words, "Life is full of appointments and disappointments, so remember only the strong succeed."

Ask yourself what your attitude would be at this point. Would you be so disappointed with how Saul's selfish spirit rubbed off on Israel's leaders that you wouldn't even want to be their king? Would you be angry at God and asking him, "How can you let this go on so long?" Or would you be tempted to say, "I gave it my best shot. It's time for me to move on to something I will enjoy more"?

When I was teaching about this season of David's life at my church, a retired airplane pilot approached me after the service. He held in his hand a note card about an important tool every pilot must learn to use before flying an aircraft. That instrument is called an attitude indicator, and every cockpit has one to help the pilot stay on course. On the indicator is a line that represents the horizon, and a small aircraft symbolizes the plane. Every pilot watches the indicator because if the nose of the airplane is too high, the engine can stall. If the nose stays too low too long, the plane will be at the wrong elevation and risk crashing. If the airplane points a little too far to the right or to the left, it will miss its destination.

How many of us have missed our destinations because we didn't understand how bad attitudes were affecting us? The writer of Hebrews warns us to "see to it that no one misses the grace of God and that no bitter root grows up to cause trouble" (12:15). Clearly, bitterness—and worry, fear, dishonor, anxiety, unbelief, and every other negative attitude—will bear different fruit in our lives than God's grace will. And it's too easy for negative feelings to take root and motivate actions we regret later on.

For instance, do you know people who married in order to get out from under their parents' authority, not because they found someone they knew they could build happy homes with? How many people have quit their jobs because they'd had it with the boss, because they didn't realize that God provided those jobs to develop in them skills they would need to succeed at places they'd enjoy more? Or how many people have given up on new relationships or new ventures because they didn't think that following God's will would be so hard? Being in God's will doesn't mean the path is easy or free of opposition.

In fact, the Bible teaches us that people who move forward in life do so because they pursue God's purposes in the hard times as well as the easy ones and even when other people's wills conflict. So sometimes it seems like we are making more progress than at other times, but the important thing is to stay on course. In 2 Samuel 3:1, we are told "the war between the house of Saul and the house of David lasted a long time. David grew stronger and stronger, while the house of Saul grew weaker and weaker." When the will of others opposes God's will in our lives, we must learn to rejoice in whatever amount of progress toward the fulfillment of his will God enables us to make.

## God's Help Versus Human Hindrance

The tug of war between God's will and human will is just one frequent battle. There's also the tug of war between God's help and human hindrance. Abner, the commander of Saul's army, was definitely a human hindrance in David's life. He had tasted the pleasures of power, and he wasn't willing to give up those pleasures without a fight even though his own life would have been better with David in charge.

It was Abner who had enough leadership influence in Israel to make Ish-Bosheth king, and Abner initiated a civil war in Israel that lasted for seven years and six months. Abner, Ish-Bosheth, and others were fighting for their own purposes, whereas David and his men fought for God.

Unfortunately, I've noticed that as I pursue God's purposes for my life, some people consider my God-ordained victory their loss. Evidently, these Abners will fight for whatever privileges come with the purposes they're pursuing. Perhaps it was David who taught his son Solomon that "jealousy [is] unyielding as the grave" (Song of Songs 8:6). David sure had a lot of people who wanted to put him in his grave!

During those times, I try to remember what God says will ultimately lead to victory or defeat:

> Don't be under any illusion: you cannot make a fool of God!
> A man's harvest in life will depend entirely on what he sows. If
> he sows for his own lower nature his harvest will be the decay
> and death of his own nature. But if he sows for the Spirit he
> will reap the harvest of everlasting life by that Spirit. Let us not
> grow tired of doing good, for, unless we throw in our hand,
> the ultimate harvest is assured. (Galatians 6:7–9, Phillips)

The ultimate harvest is assured—that's what both William Carey and David believed and acted upon. But here in Galatians we find helpful instruction for those times when the fulfillment of God's dream is delayed and we honestly feel like it may be denied. First, we can't be living under any illusion that God's purposes will fail—because they won't. Of course it's tempting to wonder when we encounter difficulties. The danger here is this: why labor for a future that doesn't appear possible? Next, we must sow actions obedient to God's Word. The Bible refers to our labor as a seed we sow, and seed determines what we'll harvest. Finally, we're told to "not grow tired of doing good," to not give up because "the ultimate harvest is assured." Here's the bottom line: faith, obedience, and patience will lead to the fulfillment of God's dream. The consistent sowing of negative emotions and sinful actions will bring a season of defeat.

Abner and Ish-Bosheth certainly experienced a season of defeat. When Abner saw the error of his ways, he sent messengers to David saying, "Whose land is it? Make an agreement with me, and I will help you bring all Israel over to you" (2 Samuel 3:12). Abner then conferred with David, and an agreement was made. But Joab, David's military commander, heard about it and shared with David his distrust of Abner. After this conversation, and acting without David's knowledge, Joab sent messengers calling Abner back to the king. Joab proceeded to take Abner aside, acting as if he wanted to speak to him privately. Joab then stabbed him in the stomach, killing him. Isn't it amazing how selfish motives have a way of backfiring on us?

Ish-Bosheth, the king exalted to the throne by man's will and enabled by man's help, couldn't sustain the loss of Abner. When he heard that Abner was dead, Ish-Bosheth "lost courage, and all Israel became alarmed" (2 Samuel 4:1). Ish-Bosheth lost courage because he knew that the people's allegiance to him was due to Abner's leadership and strength, not God's will or his rights as the sole surviving heir. The people of Israel were also concerned after their plan had failed. They wondered how David would treat those who had fought against him.

In the meantime, two of Ish-Bosheth's men, Baanah and Recab, formed a plan of their own. They went to the house of Ish-Bosheth and stabbed him in the stomach as he took his noonday rest. Then they cut off his head and took it to David saying, "Here is the head of Ish-Bosheth son of Saul, your enemy, who tried to take your life. This day the LORD has avenged my lord the king against Saul and his offspring" (2 Samuel 4:8). Again, isn't it amazing how sowing seeds from your lower nature eventually brings about decay and death—just as God said?

## GOD'S WAY AND OUR WAY

It is so important that we understand the strategies of sin. The apostle Peter warned believers to "be self-controlled and alert" because "your enemy the devil prowls around like a roaring lion looking for someone to devour" (1 Peter 5:8). Apparently Peter had also learned that a lack of caution could have dangerous consequences.

Years ago it was reported that a mountain lion was running loose in our small city. Those kinds of things do happen in rural America. According to reports one night, the lion was last spotted near our local Burger King. I wondered as I went to bed that night if most people felt a little less motivated to *have it their way*.

Have you ever wondered why God asks us to follow his way rather than our own? Is God so egocentric that he can't stand not having his own way? Or is God so controlling that he has to be in charge? Of course not. God asks us to follow his way because he knows life will go better for us if we do.

Even before being crowned king over all of Israel, David demonstrated his commitment not only to God's will but also to God's ways. That commitment helped him deal with the aftermath of Abner's death. Joab was David's military commander and a co-laborer in God's will. But he also was the conspirator who brought death to Abner. What would David do? Would he just ignore Joab's guilt because, in a sense, Abner had it coming?

No, David confronted the wrong even though it had been committed against a person who had long opposed him. He even mourned the death:

> [David] sang this lament for Abner:
> "Should Abner have died as the lawless die?
> Your hands were not bound,
> your feet were not fettered.
> You fell as one falls before wicked men."
> (2 Samuel 3:33–34)

Notice that David called Joab, his military commander, a wicked man for murdering Abner. Rather than excusing Joab's sin, David clearly stated that the murder was wrong. The Bible says, "All the people took note and were pleased; indeed, everything the king did pleased them. So on that day all the people and all Israel knew that the king had no part in the murder of Abner son of Ner" (verses 36–37).

Now remember that these men who were pleased with David were the same people who had followed Abner instead of joining Judah in making David their king. What had changed the people's hearts after seven and a half years? I believe it is the same thing that eventually changed India and that has changed the hearts of many people opposed to God's will and his ways. When God's people patiently do his will, following his ways and relying on his help—as William Carey and King David did—we win the tug of war against evil.

Obeying God's commands as he enables us—this is what it means to cooperate with God. In Philippians 2:12–13, the apostle Paul wrote the following:

> Therefore, my dear friends, as you have always obeyed—not
> only in my presence, but now much more in my absence—
> continue to work out your salvation with fear and trembling,
> for it is God who works in you to will and to act according
> to his good purpose.

God does have good purposes for all of his people, and he works in all of us to accomplish them. But notice how important our obedience is, not just when the preacher is looking, but consistently and patiently until God's will is done.

## How God Works

It took my mother more than seven years to accept my salvation experience, so I know what David went through. She was a wonderful mother; no kid in town had more loving care. (In fact, my wife wishes to this day I had been a little less spoiled!) I wasn't raised in a church like the one I now pastor. So when I gave my life to the Lord, my mom viewed it as a rejection of the lifestyle I had been raised in. I wasn't trying to reject anyone. I was simply accepting God's leadership in my life. I have since learned, as a pastor, that many people live in conflict with people they love due to their commitments to Christ.

What can we do to make peace with these loved ones and still move forward in fulfilling our God-given purposes? How can we put the past behind us and pursue a blessed future starting today? Again, David gives us insight as we look at how he unified Israel:

> All the tribes of Israel came to David at Hebron and said,
> "We are your own flesh and blood. In the past, while Saul
> was king over us, you were the one who led Israel on their
> military campaigns. And the LORD said to you, 'You will
> shepherd my people Israel, and you will become their ruler.'"
> When all the elders of Israel had come to King David
> at Hebron, the king made a compact with them at Hebron
> before the LORD, and they anointed David king over Israel.
> (2 Samuel 5:1–3)

Imagine how David felt! It had been twenty years since Samuel anointed him as king and he killed Goliath, becoming the teenage golden boy of Israel. I'm sure David had no idea that the path to the throne was going to be that hard. But I'm also sure he'd tell us now that a life characterized by resilient obedience has a satisfying reward all its own.

So please don't quit on that marriage God made you promises about! Please don't give up on that child who has been wayward for a while! And please don't give up on people giving you problems today because they might be your most loyal partners tomorrow.

Having the dream is very different from living out that dream, isn't it? Consider this bit of wisdom from a respected marriage counselor: "Love is cuddling on the sofa, but marriage is trying to earn the money to buy a sofa. Love is talking about how many kids you want to have someday, but marriage is trying to do all that's necessary to raise godly successful kids today." His point is clear—*vision is exciting, but only by enduring and doing right do we bring that vision to pass.*

At this point of David's life, he helped God's vision come to pass by making a compact with the elders of Israel. In the Bible a compact is an agreement (not a small sports car!) where the people commit to doing what God asks of them. Such agreements typically ended the death and destruction caused by individual agendas and political power games.

The spirit of this kind of agreement is what we must strive to build with other people in our own lives. We can all enter into blessed days with God if we'll help each other cooperate with God's will and his ways. When we don't cooperate in this spirit of purposeful living, then we'll stumble away from God's best for us and limp along. In order to taste the sweet flavor of a significant life, we must cooperate in ways that allow us to exercise our own unique gifts alongside others. A degree of strife and some confrontation are probably inevitable, but as long as we all work together with a cooperative spirit to achieve God's dreams, we will flourish.

# CHAPTER 11

## *Creative Detours*

Like many men, I sometimes have a hard time stopping to ask for directions. It's not that I'm too proud or too embarrassed (most of the time) but that I'd like to believe I can find my way if I just persevere and keep looking. I find driving in new places sort of like working a jigsaw puzzle. Most of the time my wife and kids are very patient with me (again, most of the time), and rather than saying, "We don't think you have a clue where we're going," they usually refer to my navigational struggles as "creative detours." Often there are silver linings to my creative detours. On a back road, we'll get a view of a beautiful sunset, or we'll discover a little hole-in-the-wall restaurant with incredible food. "Just as I planned it," I'll joke when we encounter an unexpected blessing on one of my wanderings.

The truth is, of course, that I *didn't* plan on finding those blessings.

They found us. If it were up to me, I would likely take the shortest, most efficient route between point A and point B in order to demonstrate what a wonderful sense of direction I have. But I've learned in life that if I chart my own path, solely according to my own ideas and expectations, I'm going to miss many of the blessings and opportunities God has planned for me along the way. That's one reason why we must learn to adapt to life's detours, and the key is cooperating with God and with others even during those times we feel lost. Then we won't miss out on the more significant life that only God can give.

*Cooperation is so important to significance because it determines how we'll respond when we can't see where the road ahead is taking us.* Cooperation determines whether we'll obey God and trust him and pay the price for eternal significance, or give in to our momentary frustrations. Cooperation is not merely getting along with God; it's counting the cost of following him, it's yielding and submitting to him, and it's paying the price to stay focused because you understand that he's leading you to places you could never go alone, places that will give your life greater significance than you could find on your own.

## MISTAKEN MAPS

As we think through what it means to cooperate with God during life's apparent detours, perhaps there's no better place to begin than with those maps we make for ourselves and then stubbornly follow without even considering whether they align with God's directions for our lives. Most of us have probably experienced those seasons in life when we're convinced that we know what is best for us, what will make us happy and our lives meaningful. Navigating these seasons can be like trying to drive from Maine to California using a map that's fifty years old. Our data is outdated and no longer valid. We think we know where we're going and have general plans in place, but later we find out that our own perspectives were limited.

We'll consider some of David's detours momentarily, but first I'd like to use another of my favorite stories from Scripture to illustrate what it means to live by our self-made maps. You're probably familiar with the story, a parable Jesus told while teaching about what it means to be lost and then to find your way again.

It's the tale of a wealthy man who had two sons, both of whom he loved dearly. When the younger one entered adulthood, he decided that he knew what he wanted out of life and how to get it. So he told his dad that he wanted to go ahead and receive what would one day be his—half of his father's money. Rather than saying, "Are you kidding me?" as you or I might, the father courageously handed over a wad of cash to his audacious son.

And the young man, of course, left home and headed to the big city to find a good time. (This part of the story always reminds me of Pinocchio going off to Pleasure Island to shoot pool, smoke cigars, and stay out to all hours only to find himself, like the other lost boys, turning into a donkey.) As many of us know, especially from our youth, when we have money to burn, we have no trouble finding friends to warm up around its glow. But many of us have also discovered that when the money fire grows cold, those good-timing friends are revealed as opportunists ready to move on to the next blazing party.

So our young traveler found himself broke and alone, lost and afraid. He didn't want to go back home after the way he'd treated his father, so he accepted a job as a hired-hand in charge of feeding pigs, and he often found himself so hungry that the slop he was dishing to the swine looked good.

Have you ever been so hungry that you'd eat soured milk and apple peels, spoiled fruit and scraps of food left over from dinner? Imagining this may be hard with a bounty of fast food around us, but perhaps you can relate to this young man's appetite in other ways.

You've probably never been so desperate for food that you'd eat slop, but maybe you've been willing to settle for something else less desirable than God's best. Maybe your hunger to be loved has you settling for the wrong kind of boyfriend or girlfriend. Or perhaps you're so fearful of risk that you settle for a low-paying, entry-level job rather than attempting to rise to your full potential. Perhaps an addiction has you feeding your legitimate appetite for significance with excess alcohol or other substances that can numb the pain that comes with life's detours.

But those pain-filled detours are when it can happen, when you suddenly realize where you are. You see that you were created for so much more than you've been willing to settle for. You realize that your own map is limited and that it ultimately took you into a maze of dead ends. And that realization can be a gift—as the experience of the young man in the story, better known as the prodigal son, demonstrates:

> When he came to his senses, he said, "How many of my
> father's hired men have food to spare, and here I am starving
> to death! I will set out and go back to my father and say to
> him: Father, I have sinned against heaven and against you.
> I am no longer worthy to be called your son; make me like
> one of your hired men." (Luke 15:17–19)

This young man realized that the map he drew and followed led him to starve in the pigsty. (Or, as a counselor friend of mine points out to folks in crisis, "Your best decisions led you to the place where you are now.") Our young prodigal considered another path that would perhaps restore his dignity. So he went home expecting to eat crow but instead feasted on the fatted calf!

> While he was still a long way off, his father saw him and was
> filled with compassion for him; he ran to his son, threw his
> arms around him and kissed him. (Luke 15:20)

This may be one of the most beautiful, life-giving verses in all of Scripture because, like the prodigal son, we too often underestimate our Father's compassionate love for us. No matter how lost we are because we've been following our own paths, no matter how wretched the consequences of our bad decisions, and no matter how much slop we've consumed along the way, our heavenly Father still loves us and wants us to cooperate with him. If we're willing to cooperate with him and follow his road map, if we'll choose to leave the pig trough and return to his table, he will restore us and guide us along a path leading to true significance—rather than frustration and mediocrity.

So if you're struggling with how to live a significant life, my friend, I suggest you examine your current map. So many of the disappointments and detours of life result from poor, short-sighted choices on our parts. Instead of waiting on God, we too often set out on our own, convinced that we know how to get where he wants us to go and how he wants us to get there. The good news, however, is that no matter how lost we may find ourselves, God can redirect our paths and align us with his map. If we're willing to pay the price of relinquishing the maps we sketched out and instead cooperate with him, then we will discover meaningful lives each and every day.

## MOVING TARGETS

Our own selfish desires and mistaken maps aren't the only causes of life's detours. Others are the results of unexpected delays and setbacks. Have you ever taken one of those road trips where nothing seems to go right? First it's a flat tire and no spare. Then it's a speeding ticket because you're trying to make up time lost because of the flat tire, and then the engine overheats. It's just one thing after another. Our life's journey toward significance can certainly seem to go like this as well. As we saw with the spiritual tug of war in the last chapter, sometimes we will be bombarded by the Enemy's darts in his attempts to distract and delay us. Certainly one of the most overt ways Satan tries to derail us is through persecution, temptations of all kinds, and conflicts with others.

David certainly knew something about what it meant to be a target for his enemies. As we've seen, he had to first overcome people's misconceptions of his purpose. Then he had to dodge the spears of his predecessor Saul. From there David's challenge was navigating the political maneuvers and infighting from the remnant of Saul's supporters, a group led by Abner and Ish-Bosheth and an effort complicated by Joab.

At a time when David assumed that his path to the throne was finally clear, it was suddenly even bumpier and more crowded than before. Can you relate to this kind of detour in your life, the kind where your expectations are suddenly turned upside down and the last thing you expected suddenly happens? During these times we are often most vulnerable to the Enemy's attacks. For example, you've worked hard to get that promotion: you've put in overtime, attended classes on weekends, and diligently produced exceptional work. But then someone younger than you, someone with less experience, is brought in for the position you believed had your name on it. You're tempted to either quit and take a lesser position elsewhere or else sabotage your new boss when she arrives. But perhaps God wants to use this disappointment in your life to strengthen your character and prepare you for an even greater leadership opportunity down the road.

Too often we overlook the fact that we will be persecuted in this life if we are serving God and living out his purposes for our lives. Satan is committed to pulling us away from God's path, and he will use any means he can to deter us from living a godly and significant life. That's why it's so important for us to arm ourselves with the weapons of prayer, Scripture, and fellowship with other believers. During the times when life heads in an unexpected direction, we must be willing to trust God and his sovereignty. If we don't, then we risk turning what God can use as a creative detour into a deadly pit stop.

## DIVINE DETOURS

Life's detours come about not only when we make poor choices or are attacked by the Enemy. Detours often come when our expectations don't match what God has in store for us. David encountered such a very telling little detour after he finally achieved the throne that had been promised him while he was a young shepherd boy. During a sudden lull in the action of his life, David realized that he lived in a nicer home than God did:

> After the king was settled in his palace and the LORD had
> given him rest from all his enemies around him, he said to
> Nathan the prophet, "Here I am, living in a palace of cedar,
> while the ark of God remains in a tent." (2 Samuel 7:1–2)

David felt that it was finally time to build a permanent temple for the ark of the covenant, the storage container for the Ten Commandments and the sign of God's presence with his people. Nathan confirmed to David that the Lord was with him and that God would honor David's desire with a slight variation. Rather than allowing David to build the temple, God explained—through Nathan—that he would have David's offspring be the ones to build it. It seems likely that because David was a warring king, a man of violence and bloodshed even though he was a man after God's own heart, the Lord wanted his temple constructed by a man of peace. And, if we jump ahead in the story, we know that this is in fact what happened: David's son Solomon followed him as king and built a glorious temple (1 Kings 6). How would you have responded if you were in David's place?

In Nathan's message from God was a seed of disappointment for the Shepherd King. Here David had been through so much to get to his destiny, and he thought it would be nice to build a beautiful temple and give something significant back to God. God's response conveyed overwhelming support, love, and blessing for David, but God also informed the king that he himself will not build the temple, but that his son will.

Sometimes when, like David, we reach the top of a mountain we've been climbing for a while and pause to catch our breath, we can assume that we know what God wants from us and then offer it up to him. We need to be prepared for the possibility, though, that God may not use us in the ways that we expect or wish to serve. We may be willing to serve in ministry, for instance, but what if God's setting isn't exactly what we'd imagined or wanted? As we consider what it means to embrace who we are and where God has placed us, we often have to be willing to accept that our roles may not be glamorous or in the spotlight. God may not want you to serve as senior pastor but as an usher instead. You may not lead the ministry team to Mexico, but you may be asked to organize the food drive for the local shelter.

Sometimes God-directed detours require us to lay down our gifts before God and pick up his request. These can be some of the most difficult times to cooperate with his will for our lives. We want to serve and offer up something we are motivated to give him, and yet we end up being asked to wait or to serve in a way that disappoints us. Nevertheless, we must trust that our Father knows best and we must remain humble in spirit.

Certainly David's response to this God-directed detour indicated that he knew how to be humble and grateful for what God had promised him:

> Who am I, O Sovereign LORD, and what is my family, that
> you have brought me this far?...
>
> How great you are, O Sovereign LORD! There is no one
> like you, and there is no God but you, as we have heard with
> our own ears....
>
> O LORD Almighty, God of Israel, you have revealed this
> to your servant, saying, "I will build a house for you." So your
> servant has found courage to offer you this prayer. O Sover-
> eign LORD, you are God! Your words are trustworthy, and
> you have promised these good things to your servant. Now
> be pleased to bless the house of your servant, that it may con-
> tinue forever in your sight; for you, O Sovereign LORD, have
> spoken, and with your blessing the house of your servant will
> be blessed forever. (2 Samuel 7:18, 22, 27–29)

Instead of complaining that he wouldn't get to build the temple, David realized the incredible gift he had been given. God had promised to bless him and his descendants, to remain with them (and not depart from them as he had departed from Saul), and to allow David's son to build a permanent temple. No small thing, any of these. David hadn't forgotten where he came from now that he was king. But it can be so tempting to focus on what we don't have rather than on all that we do have. A sense of entitlement can creep in, and the Enemy can use our elevated position to poison us with pride. But David provides a great example of cooperating with God even when we wish we could do it our way. His humility and gratitude should inspire us to never lose sight of what matters most.

## Praise Fuel

David's response to God here reminds me of those billboards along the interstate that tell us gas is available at the next exit. Journeying through the highways and byways of life, we can easily become sidetracked and lose our way. We can run out of gas and become exhausted and discouraged. If we dwell on our disappointments and fears, then our detours can easily turn into pit stops of bitterness and despair. Like a broken-down car abandoned on the side of the road, we will get stuck if we focus only on the pain and bruised pride of our deflated expectations.

So what can we do to replenish our fuel when life's detours drain our tanks? I'm convinced that we can make the most of any detour by looking at it as an opportunity for awe. Remember David's response to having to wait almost twenty years to ascend the throne that God had promised him when he was still a shepherd? He consistently praised God for his faithfulness and goodness. In fact, I believe David discovered one of the secrets to living a truly significant life: *praise is the fuel that keeps us moving ahead on our journeys of faith.*

Now I'm not sure if it's unleaded or regular or diesel, but I believe giving God praise, perhaps most especially when we feel lost and uncertain, keeps our heart engines running for miles and miles. Or, to make another comparison, praise sustains our focus on him as our true North Star. Like a hiker lost in the woods trying to find her bearings, we look to our Creator for perspective, a sense of where we are and where he wants to lead us next. Praise allows us to redirect our attention away from our present circumstances and wrong turns and back toward God, our hearts' best compass.

David used praise to refuel his faith tank and consult his compass in a variety of situations. Whether facing a Philistine giant, an enraged king, or a personal disappointment, David still turned toward God and gave thanks. The numerous psalms that David composed certainly testify to his ability to find reasons for awe amidst the twists and turns of his life's journey. In Psalm 145:1, he declared, "I will exalt you, my God the King; I will praise your name for ever and ever." That "for ever and ever" certainly include the disappointing times as well as the good times.

In another psalm David wrote, "Delight yourself in the LORD and he will give you the desires of your heart" (37:4). What a powerful reminder to remain focused on the joy we have in knowing God rather than on the negative self-pity that often occurs when we focus on what we don't have or didn't get. There's wisdom in David's observation as well. Basically, he instructs us to handle our life situations the way God wants us to handle them so that we can know the deepest fulfillment of our hearts' desires, not just the temporary satisfaction of getting our own way or having our fleshly desires met. I encourage you to read through the psalms. Note how many of them are praise songs and then use them as fuel for your journey.

As we conclude our look at some of God's creative detours, David's willingness to praise God in the midst of life's uncertainties and disappointments provides us with powerful examples. If we are willing to cooperate with God, he has promised to use us and fulfill us as his beloved sons and daughters. Like a tender father who loves each of his kids in a special way and gives each of them a unique task, God cares for us and desires us to be all that he created us to be. When we cooperate with him along the unexpected turns of our lives' journeys, then we can experience the blessings of creative detours, of those places that may not match our expectations but nonetheless serve as catalysts for living significant lives.

# CHAPTER 12

## Second-Story Buildings

I 'll never forget taking my wife back home to Pennsylvania shortly after we were married. We were there during the holiday season, and some friends invited us to a New Year's Eve party. We were running a little late, so the cars were already lined up in front of the house when we arrived.

My wife was surprised to see so many cars in front of what looked like such a small house. As we hurried through the chilly air and past the many cars, my wife said to me with a puzzled look: "How are all these people going to fit in this little house?" Being a Southern girl from the Texas Gulf Coast region, she didn't know that Yankee houses were often bigger than they appeared.

We rang the front door bell and were greeted by my friends. Tamara politely perused the place, looking at pictures and the beautiful items that

adorned the house, and she voiced her praise. But beneath her polite de-
meanor, I knew she was curious: where were all the guests who had parked
out front?

Finally, my friend's wife led us to the party. We walked into another
room and opened a door that led down to the basement. I wish I had a picture to remind me of how much fun it was for me to watch my wife's reaction! Food and laughter and lots of people enjoying themselves filled that
underground room.

We had a wonderful evening and joyously rang in the New Year. It was
all such fun. We so enjoyed the friends and the food and the games and the
conversation. And my enjoyment continued on the ride home.

"Ji-im," Tamara said as we got in our car. I love my wife's Southern
accent and the way she pronounces my name as if it has two syllables.

"Your parents' house doesn't have a room underground," she continued. "Do lots of houses up north have an extra room like that?"

I couldn't contain my laughter and explained to Tamara that nearly
every house in my friend's neighborhood was that way. None of the houses
were as small as they appeared. While not all of them had basements totally
concealed underground, most did have rooms beneath the main floor.
Tamara then told me that our dream house now needed to be bigger than
we'd initially planned. She definitely wanted a room just like the one she'd
just discovered!

Now, as a pastor, I'm always looking for a sermon illustration, and
when we returned to Texas, I discovered how to use this experience with a
hidden room. All of us live in two-story buildings. There's the story that we
know about ourselves and our lives—the facts, events, and history of who
we are and where we come from: where we were born, the schools we
attended, and the dates we started our present jobs. Then there's the sec-

ond story that nobody except us and God knows about unless we let them in or unless something occurs in there that becomes a tale for the outside world. *In that second-story room we handle our temptations, our successes, our failures, and our dreams—privately. Cooperation with God in this room is essential if we are to live significant lives.*

## HIDDEN ROOMS

In the struggles and strains of life, when we face temptations or have to deal with failures, however, we don't always cooperate with God. People in crisis who come to me as their pastor often tell me, "I don't know how to cooperate with God anymore, Jim. I feel like I've lost the tug of war, and now I'm just crawling along. My creative detour has become a one-way street." If we've lived life long enough and are honest about our experiences, then we know what they mean. We know what it's like to have blown it so badly that we feel like we're sliding down into a dark pit with nothing to hang on to. Perhaps an addiction to alcohol or drugs has you feeling this way. Maybe you got involved with someone sexually before marriage. Maybe you had an affair. Perhaps you had an abortion. We all have secret rooms in our personal houses, those hidden places in our lives where we didn't cooperate with God.

Even David, the man after God's own heart, the slayer of giants and the beloved king of Israel, had his secrets. And, boy, one was a real doozy! That secret kept him from cooperating with God and living a significant life until he was willing to turn back toward his Father and face what he had done. And here's what King David did.

It was spring, and that meant wartime in the ancient Middle East. David had sent General Joab off with the entire Israelite army and remained at home. That in itself was innocent enough, but it is also worthy of thought. So often when things are going well, when you finally have a little downtime after a roller-coaster ride of demanding events, you become a prime target for the snares of the Enemy. Such was the case with David. The king was bored and, I'm guessing, a little lonely:

> One evening David got up from his bed and walked around
> on the roof of the palace. From the roof he saw a woman
> bathing. The woman was very beautiful, and David sent
> someone to find out about her. The man said, "Isn't this
> Bathsheba, the daughter of Eliam and the wife of Uriah the
> Hittite?" (2 Samuel 11:2–3)

Restless, unable to sleep, strolling on the roof to appreciate the city view—all this seems harmless enough, right? Yes, but notice the sequence of events here: David went from his bed to the palace roof. He saw a beautiful woman bathing. Then he sent an attendant to find out who she was. But perhaps David should have averted his eyes as soon as he noticed a woman on the roof below him taking a bath—and, arguably, maybe she shouldn't have been bathing on her roof. But David's eyes lingered long enough to note her beauty, and he didn't stop at just admiring her beauty or even privately lusting after her. He wanted to know who she was. At that point the course of events was a slippery slope back to the king's bed—only this time he was not alone.

> Then David sent messengers to get her. She came to him,
> and he slept with her. (She had purified herself from her

uncleanness.) Then she went back home. The woman conceived and sent word to David, saying, "I am pregnant."
(2 Samuel 11:4–5)

You know about the domino effect. One topples and then another and soon an entire row has been leveled. And as we'll see in a moment as well as in the next chapter, more dominoes have yet to fall.

How could our hero, the mighty Shepherd King, with a heart of gold and a will of iron, tumble into such a messy predicament? For someone so in tune with God, David hit quite a few sour notes here. And since he was so intimately acquainted with the God who created him and anointed him as king, we have to ask, "Why would David so blatantly defy God's law and commit adultery—not to mention his choreographing the murder that came afterward?"

## BLACK ICE

Why did David sin with Bathsheba? We may never know this side of heaven what he was thinking and feeling. Being a passionate, poetic man, he may have acted impulsively out of pure desire—the desire to possess a beautiful woman, the desire to connect with someone in his loneliness, the desire for royal instant gratification. Whatever the reason for his actions, David had clearly set himself up for failure. By continuing the progression of events from point A (his initial sleeplessness in bed) to point Z (bringing another man's wife back to bed with him), David diverted from cooperating with God; the king had gotten sidetracked off the path of a significant life.

While God wants us to fulfill the desires of our hearts, he also knows what's best for us, and he established some guidelines for keeping our hearts focused on him. Now where exactly David stepped over the line is hard to say, but in this situation he clearly ran, rather than walked, across God's boundary lines. And falling into sin like this is a lot like driving on black ice. Those of you who have ever driven on roads coated with a thin glaze of ice or snow know what I mean. The slick streets look normal, but the dirty, frozen slush blends into the road to the point where it's no longer visible. If you attempt to cruise at regular speeds on a highway coated with black ice, you are setting yourself up to slide out of control.

Pause with me a moment to think about the ways we often set ourselves up for diverting ourselves away from God's best for our lives. Perhaps we allow ourselves to indulge in a shopping spree, spending money we don't have, to lift our spirits. Maybe we go to places where we know we'll stumble into trouble—the bar, the adult bookstore, the Internet, an old boy-friend's apartment. Or maybe we keep junk food on hand for a late-night binge. Why do we do it? Why can't we just say no when we're tempted to stray from God's ways?

Bottom line, of course, it's our human nature in a fallen world. We want to feel good now. We don't like suffering through painful emotions and difficult circumstances. We also set ourselves up for failure by not anticipating our true needs and by not taking care of ourselves in good ways when we're vulnerable. Many businessmen ask me to hold them accountable when they're on the road traveling. They know that they get lonely when they're away from their families and restless when they're disconnected from familiar routines. They may not eat properly or get enough sleep. So the temptations of porn or alcohol or other vices grow proportionately. Why does accountability help in these instances?

We'll unpack accountability more in the next section on community. Right now, though, it's important to realize that accountability helps by taking us to the story that people can't see; accountability makes sure that nothing wrong is happening in the basement. In the heat of the moment, when we're caught up in our own distress and loneliness, fears and discomfort, it's easy to lose sight of God's path (or "his-story," as one of my friends likes to call it) and only see the dark night before us. When we feel like all we have is what's before us, why not go for a little instant gratification? Before we find ourselves in these times, we need to understand that cooperation with God requires the very best kind of accountability—not a hand-wringing, shaming kind of police interrogation—but the kind that shares life with other people who desire God's best.

## RADICAL REDEMPTION

Now, we don't know for sure that David was lonely, bored, and lacking accountability, but those possibilities are logical enough. David certainly didn't try to stop that train of adultery once he found himself on board. And, sadly enough, he stayed on that train for a long time before realizing it was off the right track. What we learn from this chapter of David's life will help us avoid losing sight of true significance. And accountability is one way to maintain cooperation with God's plans for us.

When we've blown it and must live with the consequences, as David did with Bathsheba, we must not lose hope. The God we serve has repeatedly shown himself to be a God of radical redemption. He is able to transform the most powerful mistakes and selfish decisions into catalysts for his kingdom work. In David's situation, we see that matters got worse before they got better. Not only did David covet his neighbor's wife and commit adultery, but he then set into motion a carefully crafted plan to cover up his crimes.

David sent for Uriah the Hittite, Bathsheba's husband and a soldier in Joab's army, and gave him an unexpected furlough in hopes that he would enjoy a reunion with his wife, thereby covering up the king's paternity of her child. Uriah, however, being a diligent and devoted soldier, did not want to lose focus on his current mission or indulge in sensual pleasures such as lovemaking when his commander and fellow warriors were camping in tents.

Probably frustrated but clearly undeterred in his cover-up, David then sent his lover's husband back to the front lines with a letter to Joab requesting that Uriah be placed in harm's way. Sure enough, David's plan worked, and the Hittite died in battle. The king could now marry Uriah's widow without anyone knowing his secrets:

> When Uriah's wife heard that her husband was dead, she
> mourned for him. After the time of mourning was over,
> David had her brought to his house, and she became his
> wife and bore him a son. But the thing David had done
> displeased the LORD." (2 Samuel 11:26–27)

So the dominoes continued to topple in this season of David's life, as if his secret room had turned into an entire maze of lies and deceit. From that restless night when he found himself up on his roof looking down on the lovely woman bathing to conceiving a child with her to his execution of her husband to marrying her—one bad choice led to another—and to so many powerful consequences. But after Uriah's death and David's marriage to Bathsheba, David was home free, right? After all, no one knew what he had done.

Wrong! Even if Joab and Bathsheba didn't suspect something fishy there, the Lord clearly knew the heart of this man whom he had called and anointed to be king over his people. And he was not happy. God's unhappiness is so important to remember when we find ourselves tempted to follow our own counsel and go down our own paths. We may be able to fool everyone else, to lie and deceive, cover up and conspire against. We may even be able to convince ourselves that what we did was justified. In this case, for instance, David was the king. Shouldn't he have everything—and everyone—he wanted? But God knew for David and he knows for us what's really going on. No matter how great a spin we put on our stories, no matter how many ways we try to make our basements into ballrooms, God sees the *real* story.

The Lord knows when we fall away and venture out on our own trails, hoping to find something besides him to satisfy us. And, amazingly enough, even when we run away and refuse to cooperate with his plans, he still manages to produce an amazing redemption from our rebellion. He does this in two ways.

First, God allows our decision-making disasters to become opportunities for us to realize how much he loves us and desires to work through us. Like the compassionate father pacing up and down the driveway as he waits for his wayward child to come home, God is always there, waiting for us to return. And when we do, rather than condemning us and punishing us as we deserve (and as we sometimes even wish he would!), he bathes us in his loving mercy, accepting us because of the bridge made by the death of his Son on the cross. Our Father in heaven loves us so much more than we realize, and that love never wavers, let alone stops, when we mess up.

And, upon our return, God restores us and builds us up again, transforming us into the people he created us to be.

In the next chapter we'll look at David's restoration, but right now I'm going to jump ahead in his story in order to illustrate the second way God brings about redemption in our lives: God does so by harvesting the fruit of the seeds we sow. Even, for example, when we sow wild oats—as David did with Bathsheba—God uses those seeds to yield a harvest for his kingdom.

To see exactly how God does this in David's story, we must fast-forward through several generations to the gospel of Matthew. There, Matthew recounts the genealogy of the Messiah, including, "David was the father of Solomon, whose mother had been Uriah's wife" (1:6). In other words, the king's adulterous affair with Bathsheba, a woman he married after having her husband killed, was transformed into a vehicle for eventually producing God's Son. Bathsheba not only brought Solomon, the next king of Israel and the builder of the temple, into the world; she also furthered the bloodline leading to Christ. (You'll recall that in the Christmas story Joseph and Mary had to go to Bethlehem during the census because he belonged to the house and line of David.)

And while we're looking at Matthew's genealogy, please note another woman listed there. In verse 5, we're reminded that Rahab, a former prostitute, was the mother of Boaz, who married the widow Ruth and continued the lineage of the Messiah. Amazing, isn't it? Our redeemer God took those flawed people and used their mistakes to accomplish his plans—and today he still delights in transforming lives when we're willing to cooperate with him.

God's willingness and ability to redeem our mistakes do not, however, give us license to exploit his grace. Paul made this very clear in Romans: "Shall we go on sinning so that grace may increase? By no means! We died to sin; how can we live in it any longer?" (6:1–2). However, neither should we despair or ever feel beyond his reach. He is a God of second chances—and of third and fourth and 1,983,524th chances!

## ONE LINK AT A TIME

Maybe you're thinking, *I believe you, Jim. I know that God gives second chances to everyone. But you don't realize how badly I've blown it.* If you struggle with seeing how God can redeem some of the messes of your life—perhaps even one you're in right now—then let me remind you of what he asks of us. First, while we would like everything to change overnight—for the consequences and hurts of our selfish decisions to magically and instantly reverse themselves—that's not how our Father operates. And, second, he doesn't ask us to operate that way either. He doesn't expect us to change overnight and instantly become perfect. Instead, he asks us to cooperate with him one moment, one hour, one day at a time, like links in the long chain of destiny. I know that phrase *one day at a time* might sound cliché, but isn't it encouraging to realize that we don't have to accomplish the impossible? Doing the impossible is God's job. We only have to cooperate with him in each moment.

Now, as I've shared, I'm something of a history buff, intrigued by the stories of famous men and women who shaped and experienced world-changing events. One of my favorites is Winston Churchill, the great British Prime Minister who battled Hitler's Nazi forces in World War II and held his country together until the Allied victory was secured. Churchill knew what it was like to face overwhelming fear and impossible odds. I'm sure that during the Blitz of London, it must have looked like his country would be destroyed and plundered. But Churchill kept focusing on one step each day. He lived out the wisdom he expressed in this statement: "We make a great mistake in not handling destiny one event at a time."

God asks no more of us than to accept the challenges of today's link, promising that if we cooperate with him, we will forge a partnership that's guaranteed to succeed. If we will turn away from our secret rooms and dark basements, and if we will come into the light, God will reveal the true story of our significance. We can rest in his loving arms no matter what we've done, and we can move into a destiny that he has already redeemed.

So, as we conclude our section on cooperation, I encourage you to realize what's at stake. *If you genuinely desire to live a significant life, a life with an eternal contribution to God's kingdom, a life filled with the joy of knowing you're becoming all that your Father created you to be, then consider the areas in your life where you struggle to cooperate with him.* Whether you are involved in a spiritual tug of war, or barricading yourself in the darkness of your own secret sins, or feeling lost and forgotten on one of life's creative detours, or doing a combination of all three, it's never too late. Turn toward the ultimate power source. Give yourself to him each day, knowing that your divine destiny is a joint effort, a cooperative endeavor, in which you are privileged to participate. And with each step of the journey, you'll discover the joy and peace that come from cooperating with the Author of true significance.

# PART V

# Community

*How good and pleasant it is
when brothers live together in unity!...
For there the LORD bestows his blessing,
even life forevermore.*

PSALM 133:1, 3

# CHAPTER 13

## *Self Service*

Perhaps you saw the recent Academy Award–winning documentary *March of the Penguins*. In this fascinating film, the annual journey of emperor penguins from the coastal ocean waters of Antarctica to their inland breeding grounds reveals much about the intricate design of God's amazing creation. One of these creatures' most striking characteristics is the way they interact as a group, particularly during the harsh subzero winters when their eggs are incubating.

During these bitter months of snow, ice, and frigid cold, the emperor penguin parents take turns balancing their single egg on the tops of their feet, under their bellies. However, in order for any of the eggs and parents to survive the brutal conditions, the colony of several thousand birds instinctively forms a large, jostling mass. They know that if any of them are to endure, if their colony and species are to survive, they must help one another stay warm. So, in their black and white huddle, they seem to constantly move, shifting and turning, bumping and stretching—somewhat like an energetic crowd of fans at a rock concert. The penguins move like that in order to keep their body temperatures high enough to endure the ruthless Antarctic winter.

As we explore the concept of community, the final factor that contributes to a significant life, I can't help but think about these emperor penguins. Many of us know that we need other people just like those penguins need one another, yet we still struggle in our relationships. So, in our final section, I'd like to examine what it means to live a significant life in community, how to overcome barriers to becoming a strong community of significance, and what to do in order to leave a legacy that echoes throughout eternity.

## Separate Igloos

As I watched *March of the Penguins,* it occurred to me that if emperor penguins acted more like people, the species would probably be extinct! They would have had several civil wars, splintered into dozens of separate groups, and seen many individuals go off on their own only to struggle to make it alone. Some of the penguins would live in separate igloos with security fences surrounding their turf. They wouldn't know one another very well, and they certainly wouldn't admit to needing one another.

I'm exaggerating, of course, but after watching the film, I did find myself wondering why it is so hard for people to participate in community. There's no getting away from the fact that God made us relational beings.

Since the creation of Adam and Eve in the garden, God has made it clear that we need other humans to overcome the loneliness that exists even when we're in paradise, even when we're in perfect relationship with our Father. Throughout history and throughout Scripture, the concept of community is clearly important to our Creator. Whether community takes the shape of a small remnant, such as Noah's family on the ark, or of a large nation, such as the children of Israel, community offers numerous benefits, including survival and safety, identity and cultural tradition, and service and success.

Yet in the early twenty-first century, finding a healthy, genuine community to be a part of has become a challenge. We'll consider some specific obstacles to community building in our next chapter, but I believe the fundamental challenge is simply us and our focus on our own individual happiness—or at least on what we think will make us happy. Especially in America, the emphasis historically has been on the power of the individual to make a better life for himself or herself. But even as countless people enjoy individual prosperity, scores of people are seeking an answer to relational separation and pain.

Despite our personal achievements, we live unsatisfied until our accomplishments are experienced within a significant community. As a pastor, I minister to people in tremendous pain despite the fact that they belong to a good church and live with a large family in a nice house that is part of a lovely neighborhood. *For all our external successes, we may not be living significant lives because we're not sharing them with others, because we're not building community.*

In fact, I'm afraid that our twenty-first century has become a perilous time for community building. On one hand, we have amazing technology that enables us to trade e-mails with pen pals in South Africa, send instant messages to friends a thousand miles away, or visit with people sharing common interests in dozens of Internet chat rooms. The global community is larger and more plugged in than ever before.

On the other hand, all of this time we spend plugged in—with cell phones, BlackBerry devices, laptops, pagers, PDAs, and wireless technology—means that we're bombarded with information and messages. I once counted the number of e-mails I received in a week. I included junk and spam as well as personal and ministry-related e-mails, and the number was well over one hundred! That is lot to me, and yet I know that many of you receive more than that in one day!

What effect does this information overload and technological exhaustion have on how we view community? These days all of us can stay in touch with one another all the time. But this capability doesn't ensure that we know how to build a strong, vital, God-honoring community. In fact, we're so tired at the end of the day that we often just want to hibernate in our homes and veg in front of the television with our immediate family. It's hard to want to participate in another meeting or group function when we have no downtime.

Perhaps this exhaustion helps explain a phenomenon I frequently encounter at our church. Many people have told me that they like participating in a larger church because they can slip in and out anonymously. They can worship, absorb the teaching, and enjoy some casual fellowship with old and new acquaintances. But they don't have to go below those surface connections and get to know people at a deeper level. Consequently, they don't let their real needs be known or reveal more than "Fine" when asked how they're doing. They also don't feel required to serve others and get involved in people's lives. While this kind of "church lite" may be fine for a limited season of rest and renewal, it's not the way God intends for us to live. That's not a picture of Christian community; it's not his design for his church body.

Knowing about this temptation to attend church anonymously, my team and I at Faith Family Church have worked to ensure that everyone who visits has the opportunity to move beyond a casual welcome and experience more significant community. As we've grown from several hundred to a few thousand, our church has begun to offer different ways for people to go below the surface and get plugged in. We try to make sure that newcomers are shepherded by a church leader who can help them find a small group, a Bible study, a personal resource, or whatever it is they need. Ours is not a perfect system by any means, but we're doing our best to let individuals know that they are what matters, not big numbers or beautiful facilities. While there's nothing wrong with having a megachurch on a lovely campus, we must never lose sight of the fact that people make up the church and every other community of significance.

## HAVE IT YOUR WAY

Other than being exhausted and overextended, what else keeps people from wanting to invest in other people, whether at church or where they live? (Think for a moment about how many of your neighbors you know. If you're like many of us, it's difficult enough to learn their names, let alone who they really are and how they're actually doing.) Underlying the many dynamics that influence how we relate to others is one fundamental challenge: Am I willing to sacrifice some of my individual freedom for what we can experience together? And am I willing to conform to other people's standards in order to belong?

I most recently observed this tug of war between desire for community and desire for independence as our kids became teenagers, beginning to leave the nest and trying their own wings. In many ways they want the security of still being a kid, of knowing that Tamara and I are there for them, taking care of them, and loving them. Yet in other ways they want to be their own persons, thinking for themselves, making independent choices, and doing their own things. Though this tug of war is a natural part of growing up, it's painful nonetheless.

To one degree or another, we all continue to experience this pull between community and independence throughout our lives. We want the group security as well as the sense of identity and belonging, yet we want the freedom to have our own way. But having it our own way carries a cost. When we have to choose between the welfare of the community versus what we want right now, we face an incredible struggle. Unfortunately, we often try to pretend that our individual choices don't really affect anyone else. We try to justify our decisions and find loopholes in the rules and regulations that make us the exception. It's like a good friend once told me, "I believe in the speed limit except when I'm in a hurry!"

Perhaps there's no better example of an individual choice affecting lots of other people than David's encounter with Bathsheba. That choice, like so many selfish choices, in one "me moment" caused hundreds of ripples across the water of community. I'm sure you can recall the sordid events in this story that sounds like a modern soap opera: while his armies were away at battle, David wandered up to his rooftop one night, saw a gorgeous woman bathing, sent for her, slept with her, conceived a child with her, and then had her husband killed and married her to cover up his crime.

Clearly, our positions, titles, privileges, or ranks can't squelch our inclinations to serve ourselves. Even if we're kings or presidents, CEOs or chairs of the local ladies' auxiliary, we're still prone to wanting our own ways. I'm afraid to say, however, that as we advance in life, we sometimes lose sight of this basic truth about the self-centeredness of human nature. All of us are going to face temptations, and what we do in response to these opportunities to serve ourselves will often have a lot to do with whether we enjoy community or simply endure it.

David's privileged situation, for instance, allowed him to lose sight of what was most significant in his life. As a victorious and beloved king, David could apparently do whatever he wanted, and up to this point in his life, he did most things right. David honored God, fought battles, resisted the chance to murder Saul, and united factions to bring together a nation that would serve the Lord. But with Bathsheba, David encountered another kind of battle, and he failed. The ripples of his failure spread out further and further. David was not just an adulterer; he was also a murderer. But he was not just a murderer; he was lying to God and to himself, not to mention to all the people he served.

We see David's selfishness and its consequences on a large scale, but I suspect most of us can identify with this kind of ripple effect even if our crimes are smaller. When we sin, its effects often spiral out of control. We tell a little lie, for example, and then need to cover up that lie when somebody else asks us what happened. When we lie, we feel bad, which often only serves to make us act out some more. For example, we work hard to suppress our guilt, or we try to make others think we're doing all right. Or, because we can't handle the fact that we've failed, we indulge our selfishness: we throw ourselves into our behavior, wallow in it, and feel it just can't be overcome. Whichever response we choose, our solution is all about ourselves, and we erode the possibility of community because the foundation of trust with God and with people has been damaged.

## THE ROYAL ME

Truth has a way of rising to the top, though, especially when God is at the center of the community—as he should be. In David's case, God sent the prophet Nathan to speak the truth. You'll recall that the prophet Samuel anointed David king in the first place. Another prophet of God told David's predecessor Saul that he was going to be removed from the throne. In this case, God sent exactly the kind of person to David that we all need when we lose sight of how our lives intersect with others': God sent a godly person who willingly and boldly spoke the truth.

But Nathan was wise enough to know that David, like most of us, really didn't want to hear the plain, unvarnished truth. So Nathan told the king a story:

> There were two men in one city, one rich and the other poor. The rich man had exceedingly many flocks and herds. But the poor man had nothing, except one little ewe lamb which he had bought and nourished; and it grew up together with him and with his children. It ate of his own food and drank from his own cup and lay in his bosom; and it was like a daughter to him. And a traveler came to the rich man, who refused to take from his own flock and from his own herd to prepare one for the wayfaring man who had come to him; but he took the poor man's lamb and prepared it for the man who had come to him. (2 Samuel 12:1–4, NKJV)

David was outraged by the story and declared that the rich man must surely pay for such a bold and brazen crime. To rob someone is wrong in and of itself, but for one who has plenty to steal from another who has only one seems especially unfair. When David declared that the rich man must die, Nathan delivered the punch line to his king: "You are the man!" (verse 7).

Nathan's story delivered truth quite effectively, didn't it? It's important to recognize the power of a well-crafted story because when we cover our selfishness with layers of denial and justification, it can be difficult for the truth about what we've done to penetrate our hearts. We become callous and indifferent to the needs of other people as well as to the ways that God would have us both serve them and receive from them. When we're busy trying to cover up past crimes, we're also unable to imagine the redemptive work God could do in our situations. No wonder the truth often has to sneak up on us in order to truly be absorbed.

Such was the case with David, for after Nathan revealed the point of his story about the ewe lamb, he went on to reveal what God had to say about David's circumstances:

> Why did you despise the word of the LORD by doing what is evil in his eyes? You struck down Uriah the Hittite with the sword and took his wife to be your own. You killed him with the sword of the Ammonites. Now, therefore, the sword will never depart from your house, because you despised me and took the wife of Uriah the Hittite to be your own.
>
> This is what the LORD says: "Out of your own household I am going to bring calamity upon you. Before your very eyes I will take your wives and give them to one who is close to you, and he will lie with your wives in broad daylight. You did it in secret, but I will do this thing in broad daylight before all Israel." (2 Samuel 12:9–12)

The truth is painful. Nobody wants to be called a liar, an adulterer, or a cheater. Nobody wants to be dethroned from the little kingdoms we build for ourselves. We also don't want to see the messy consequences of our selfishness. We don't want to acknowledge the terrible pain and suffering our decisions have caused other people. And we certainly don't want to face the disappointment of our loving Father.

Yes, what God said to David regarding his failures may sound harsh, but as we saw when we time-traveled in the previous chapter, there was redemption. Perhaps those severe consequences were necessary for David to realize that his relationship with God and with his community needed to matter more to him than his own desires did. Whatever the reason for the severity of the consequences, the truth about David's actions left a wide wake in its path when it finally surfaced. In his beautiful and moving prayer of Psalm 51, we see that David did repent and acknowledge that he had sinned foremost against God.

> For I acknowledge my transgressions,
>> And my sin is always before me.
> Against You, You only, have I sinned,
>> And done this evil in Your sight—
>> That You may be found just when You speak,
>> And blameless when You judge....
>
> Create in me a clean heart, O God,
>> And renew a steadfast spirit within me....
>
> Restore to me the joy of Your salvation,
>> And uphold me by Your generous spirit.
>> (Psalm 51:3–4, 10, 12, NKJV)

Before we can come clean with others, we must come clean before God. Too often, though, we lose sight of the fact that he is the One we fail the most when we choose our selfish desires over his ways. And perhaps we find it difficult to ask others to forgive us when we haven't experienced the grace and mercy of God's forgiveness, made possible through the gift of his Son.

What areas of your life do you need to change in order to serve God more faithfully? What secrets weigh you down and prevent you from living the fullness of the significant life for which you were created? I encourage you to take these matters before God. Let him know what's on your heart. Remember that he loves you and wants to lead you into an abundant life filled with his blessings and joy. But first you have to let go of the ways in which you have tried to serve yourself before him and others.

## TEAMMATES AND TERMITES

Maybe there's no secret sin in your life or large weight holding you back, but you still struggle with investing in community. You may be dealing with what I believe is another manifestation of our selfishness. What's your basic attitude toward the purpose of your participation in community? Too often it's easy to focus solely on what others can do for us, on the ways that the community can serve us, rather than on what we are called and gifted to contribute to a community.

I hate to make generalizations, especially at the risk of being corny, but I've found that most folks fall into one of two categories in their approaches to community. They either serve as teammates, those who want to work with others to produce something great, or as termites, those who want to consume the community for their own personal benefits.

We all know that termites are those nasty little bugs that get into our wooden structures and destroy our homes and buildings. We usually don't even realize they're present until the foundation starts crumbling. The same can be true about those people in our community who are more committed to themselves than to others. They may be invisible in the group until they need to give to the people around them. The community collapses when those people drain its resources but give nothing in return.

Teammates, however, always have a larger goal in mind—the good of the team. I love the story of Joe Gordon, once a third baseman for the New York Yankees. One day a newspaper reporter asked Joe's manager, Joe McCarthy, which player he most liked managing. Rather than answering, McCarthy turned around and called out Gordon's name. Gordon ran over to the bench, and McCarthy asked him some questions:

"Joe," McCarthy asked, "what's your batting average?"

"I don't know," the player said.

"How many RBIs have you got?"

Gordon shrugged. "Don't know."

"What *do* you know, Joe?"

"I know we're playing Boston, and I know we're playing to win."

His point clearly illustrated, McCarthy looked up at the reporter and smiled. Compared to today's world of professional athletes, Gordon's attitude seems all the more remarkable and refreshing. It's so easy for pro athletes today to become celebrities who are fixated on personal statistics and looking for their next million-dollar endorsement. Such people, whether athletes or everyday people, are termites. They are all about me, me, me, and they usually destroy the foundation of a good team. In sharp contrast, Joe Gordon was a teammate. Teammates see something worth striving for beyond stats and outward appearances. They play to win, and if we're going to play to win, we have to understand what it means to be part of something larger than ourselves with a goal greater than our own momentary happiness.

One of the blessings that came out of the terrible ordeal of Hurricane Katrina was witnessing the way so many diverse people came together, united by the cause of helping others. Our church in Texas had the opportunity to help many displaced families from neighboring Louisiana, and we can certainly testify that it brought many special blessings of the heart. We received, for example, a fresh understanding of what we miss when we are consumed by doing our own thing instead of making time to meet others' legitimate needs. We also became more deeply aware of how investing in others is essential to living lives of significance. Every day each one of us has opportunities to be a teammate, and we must seize those moments and invest in others intentionally if we want to reap the rewards of community.

So, before we move on and consider some of the problems and conflicts that inevitably arise in community, I encourage you to reflect on your current relationships. Which people in your life do you truly feel called to love and serve? Which areas of your life do you need to address in order to more fully honor God and to more capably serve others? Would you rather be a termite or a teammate—and which category are you in today?

As we've seen throughout our exploration in this book, significant living basically boils down to fully embracing who God has created you to be and living by the principles of his kingdom. *If we aren't using what God has given us for more than our own pleasure and well-being, then we will eventually find ourselves empty and disappointed.* As Jesus reminded us, "What good will it be for a man if he gains the whole world, yet forfeits his soul?" (Matthew 16:26). True community begins when, recognizing the significance of other people, we serve them and love them—and let them serve and love us—in ways that will endure for generations to come.

# CHAPTER 14

## Four-Wheel Drive

My friend Ron heard God's call into full-time ministry at an early age. But in his small rural town he struggled to find people who shared his passion for missions. When he went away to college, he thought he would finally find a band of individuals headed in the same spiritual direction. Instead, he discovered a party attitude held by most students, including the Christians. Disappointed, he nevertheless managed to find a few like-minded friends but not the larger community he'd hoped for.

Finally, Ron graduated and was accepted at a prominent, Bible-based seminary. He was so happy to sense God's leading to this well-respected and Christ-centered institution. One of the things he anticipated most was the experience of community that he knew must exist among those on campus—his fellow students, the faculty and staff, and their spouses and families. He just knew that the seminary would be a tremendous place of growth and encouragement where he could forge lifelong friendships.

As you might guess, community life on the grounds of this seminary certainly stimulated growth, but unfortunately not to the degree Ron had counted on. Other than a few peers with whom he studied, he discovered that no one really had time for relationships. Competition for the student preaching awards seemed to keep most seminarians at arm's length from one another. Faculty members were good teachers, but they were far too busy with grading, research, and committee work to mentor individual students. Staff members were nice, but they seemed caught up in their own responsibilities and relationships with one another.

Ron told me that this time at seminary was one of the most disappointing seasons of his life. "I thought I'd finally discover what it means to experience true community," he said. "Instead, I found just another busy place where people were all doing their own thing." I'm afraid that experiences like these leave lasting impressions that determine how we view community, and from what I can tell, many people today don't expect much from those around them anymore. They just assume people are too busy or are already caught up in other relationships.

Can you relate? How would you describe your participation in the group you presently think of as your community? Has there ever been a time when you expected to fit into a group only to discover that the people inside the group weren't very connected to one another at all?

## SPOKES ON THE WHEEL

From my observations, Ron's not alone in both his search for and disappointment with participating in community. As we discussed last chapter, it can be so difficult in our high-speed wireless world to slow down and really connect with people. But I remain convinced that community is essential if we are to lead fulfilling and significant lives. We can have all the money in the world, mansions as big as football fields, titles and privileges of the elite, and still feel empty and disconnected from real relationships.

*The truth is that without the stage of community upon which to stand, we can't achieve the fullness of true significance.* Jesus consistently reminds us that true significance grows within community. We experience soul significance when we link ourselves to people around us, giving and receiving, struggling and surviving, rejoicing and encouraging.

One of my favorite images for this community process is a wagon that once belonged to the grandfather of an older gentleman in our church. The worn and weathered wagon bed is supported by four large wheels, each with a center hub, dozens of spokes, and an outer metal rim. With the four wheels in place, the wagon could roll for miles and miles—or until the horses and mules got tired.

Those rustic wagon wheels serve as simple yet powerful symbols of how significant communities operate. At the hub, we find the group's common goals and shared values. We Christians place God and his will in the center of the wheel: we seek to know and share his leading both individually and corporately.

Extending from the hub are the numerous spokes that connect the center to the rim of the wheel. Although we don't often see spokes on the wheels of our modern vehicles, I'm guessing most of you have seen these wooden dowel-type spokes that I'm describing. In order to be effective community members, we must serve like the spokes on a wheel. We must be strong and united, working individually to connect what's most important to us (the hub) with our actions (the outer rim that shows how our community rolls along). One missing spoke will weaken the entire wheel and slow down the movement. When too many spokes are broken or missing, the wheel itself breaks down under the weight of what it's bearing.

So how do we turn just another busy place into a significant community, a body of people involved in ministry to the world and one another, a group with four-wheel drive for the kingdom? In order to build a community that collectively grows in its pursuit of God's best and not just in pursuit of size, status, or wealth, I believe we must adopt four strategies. First, we must *prioritize* our community commitments, focusing on where God has placed us and with whom we interact on an ongoing basis. Next, we need to *practice* compassionate communication with people in our community; we need to learn how to deal with conflict and how to extend healthy, effective accountability. In the midst of the inevitable conflicts and tensions, we must *pursue* forgiveness and grace. And, finally, in order to grow deep roots in the soil of community, we should patiently *persevere* throughout the variety of seasons common to every community.

Most communities seem to thrive when these four core values—focus, communication, forgiveness, and perseverance—are practiced regularly. When that's the case, the result is a four-wheel-drive vehicle that moves efficiently, overcomes rough terrain, and transports individuals to destinations they could never reach by themselves. By prioritizing our commitments, practicing honest communication, pursuing forgiveness, and persevering with one another over the bumps of life, we can—along with God's help—overcome almost any obstacle. So let's look more closely at these four wheels.

## SUPERHEROES FLY SOLO

As we saw in the preceding chapter, one of the foremost obstacles to community is the need to get over ourselves and acknowledge that we need other people. I think if we're honest, deep down we long to have significant relationships, rich connections to other people. And that makes sense since we are created in God's image: we are made to be relational beings just as he is. Those of us sharing the bonds of the Christian faith know that we need one another if we are to grow and become the people God calls us to be.

On the other hand, I'm guessing that we've all experienced our share of disappointments, betrayals, and losses so we're tempted to avoid getting too close or too attached to other people. Like my friend Ron, we've been frustrated by our longing to connect and the reality of what people offer. Or, worse still, we have learned firsthand what it's like when those whom we trust turn against us and hurt us. Past wounds and still-tender scars may mean we have to work to rebuild our ability to trust.

But our Lord knows this. Jesus told us, "A new command I give you: Love one another. As I have loved you, so you must love one another" (John 13:34). Even though at times it may seem impossible to love people, it's what God has called us to do: to show others the same grace and mercy that he extends to us. If we don't obey this command, we miss out on two major categories of significance: serving others and being served by them. While it may seem like none of us can ignore the people in our lives, I believe this solitary attitude exists as a definite and destructive mind-set, one that I call the superhero syndrome.

I gave it that name because of a insightful observation my son Geoffrey once made. We were visiting with some friends over dinner while the kids watched television and played games. Just as we were finishing dessert, Geoffrey, who loved Buzz Lightyear at the time, raced over and said, "I don't think I want to be a superhero anymore." I smiled and asked, "Why's that?" He looked up at me and said, "They have to fly alone." And with that comment he raced off to join the rest of the group.

There's wisdom in Geoffrey's conclusion: superheroes fly solo. When you try to do everything for yourself and for those you love, then you're functioning according to the false belief that you can be Superman or Wonder Woman. Many of you reading this are probably very good at being a superhero: you're organized, disciplined, focused, and incredibly detail oriented. You chauffeur the kids to practice after school, help them with their homework, pick up the dry cleaning, cook dinner, make extra servings to take to the new neighbors, and then pay the bills while you listen to a sermon series on your iPod. Whew! The list makes me tired just thinking about it!

Or, on the other extreme, you're feeling guilty because you've tried to do it all and know that you can't. Yet you're still trying, still striving, and still comparing yourself to others. In either case, you're missing something central to the truth about living a significant life in community: *we can't do it by ourselves—and we don't have to.*

The key to overcoming as well as avoiding the superhero syndrome is to commit to other people, and that means both giving to them of your authentic self and receiving from them what they offer you. And this kind of connection requires trust. When I talk about this with people struggling to avoid Lone Ranger living, they often tell me that they're uncertain whom they should include in their community commitments, whom to trust with the deeper levels of their lives.

Ideally, of course, this decision hinges not just on the proximity of people, but on shared priorities. In fact, by definition, communities are united around common causes and goals. Once, a long time ago, the main goal was simply staying alive and providing food and shelter and safety for one another. From there, communal goals developed into the diverse objectives we see groups pursuing today—everything from political policy to animal rights, from athletic endeavors to flea-market finds. (With the numerous and varied groups to which we can all belong, it's no wonder many people struggle to prioritize their memberships!)

As a nation we experienced incredible unity after September 11, 2001, when people came together to grieve, to comfort one another, to suffer and mourn as a country that was suffering like never before. Suddenly political, social, and ethnic differences were laid aside, and we were deeply connected with compassion and concern for one another.

When a crisis like this occurs, it reminds us of what's most important to us. Then, at least for a while, we're able to lay aside our prideful independence and unite with others. But it need not take such tragedies as Katrina or 9/11 to remind us that we need one another. We must simply hold on to the truth that real significance comes only with living in a community committed to larger goals than any one person can accomplish alone.

As I've stated, I recommend choosing your primary community by looking at your priorities. Certainly, we all have families, friends, and co-workers, and our families have always served as our primary community. And it comes as no surprise that I believe it's important to belong to a strong faith community as well. Nevertheless, depending on the season of our lives, God may want us more heavily invested in other communities. For some, that community might be a ministry or parachurch organization, a charitable institution, or a community-service group.

## No Spare Parts

Regardless of which community you feel called to invest in, it's vital that you don't try to spread yourself too thin and that you serve where you're planted rather than where you may wish you'd been planted. After all, part of being willing to commit to others is recognizing what you have to give and what you need. As followers of Jesus, we are to be committed to people who are our brothers and sisters in God's family. We want to show them the love of Christ and help one another grow into our full, God-given potential. At times in this pursuit, though, we can be easily tempted to wish that we were like someone else, that we had that person's gifts or abilities rather than our own. At these times, it's important to remember that each one of us has been gifted uniquely. God doesn't make mistakes, so whatever he's given us is what he wants us to give to others. When we compare ourselves to fellow believers and try to be people we're not, we lose sight of our own significance and we lose our focus on the well-being of others.

In the church, we are to realize that we are each part of the body of Christ, reminded by Paul that we all serve unique functions. Some serve as eyes, some as hands, and others as the mouth or feet:

> Now the body is not made up of one part but of many. If the foot should say, "Because I am not a hand, I do not belong to the body," it would not for that reason cease to be part of the body. And if the ear should say, "Because I am not an eye, I do not belong to the body," it would not for that reason cease to be part of the body. If the whole body were an eye, where would the sense of hearing be? If the whole body were an ear, where would the sense of smell be? But in fact God has arranged the parts in the body, every one of them, just as he wanted them to be. If they were all one part, where would the body be? As it is, there are many parts, but one body. (1 Corinthians 12:14–20)

As we see here, there are no spare or unnecessary parts. God uses each of us in special ways. So, basically, we must appreciate our differences and accept the gifts we've been given rather than try to be something we're not.

I've learned this lesson again and again on the baseball field. Often, for instance, a guy who was strong and had great potential as a hitter focused on trying to be a pitcher, something he wasn't cut out for. Despite his strength, the speed and accuracy of his pitches never developed. Yet he couldn't let go of his dream to be a pitcher, so he missed the opportunity to be a great hitter and fielder.

Letting go of who we aren't can often be more difficult than embracing who we are. But it's part of the process of committing to and trusting both God and others so that we can play our roles in community life. David certainly faced these issues of trust and commitment throughout his lifetime. When he trusted God and worked in harmony with others, God used David to produce acts of eternal significance: David defeated a giant against impossible odds, navigated treacherous political terrain, united a fractured group of warring tribes, and established a plan for building God's temple.

On the other hand, when David wavered and set off on his own path, his mistakes produced flat tires, impeding the progress of his community. Primarily, his lack of self-control with Bathsheba and, as we'll see momentarily, with his own family, particularly his son Absalom, created tremendous turmoil within the nation of Israel as well as within David himself.

This hindsight view of this great man's life further emphasizes one of the fundamentals of community: what we do as individuals affects other people. When we refuse to acknowledge our need for others and at the same time withhold what we have to offer them, we fail to become all that God made us to be. Like ripples in a pond when a single stone breaks the calm surface, our actions powerfully impact the lives of others in a variety of ways. One simple act of kindness can change the direction of another person's day, week, or even lifetime.

## FREEDOM OF SPEECH

Honest communication is another aspect of community building which, like the others, requires ongoing practice in order to keep the wheels greased and rolling smoothly. And honest communication is one of the toughest skills to practice. It involves an ongoing effort to take risks and conquer fears about, for instance, how others might misunderstand us and what they may think of us. Honest communication also means resisting the temptation to manipulate and control, gossip and slander. In order to communicate effectively within community, three dynamics are absolutely necessary: trust, safety, and consistency.

First, besides being central to the way we prioritize our commitments, trust is equally essential for honest and effective communication. Without trust as the foundation of a relationship, we find it difficult to go below the surface and reveal our hearts and our struggles. Without trust, the community will grow only so close, and then interpersonal connections plateau in polite exchanges of data. Trading information is part of communication, but real communication goes far beyond just the words that are exchanged. Authentic connections require that we hear what is *not* said—what is implied by the tone and style of the message and how we think it was intended.

Trust can be difficult to build especially after it has been ruptured by betrayal. And we certainly don't need to trust everyone to the same degree. Trust is a gift to be earned, not something to which anyone is automatically entitled. So be careful about how vulnerable you are with people; listen to your heart and to God's voice for guidance about what to share with whom and when. Even when we're careful and discerning, we will probably still experience some disappointment and frustration. However, if our trust is foremost in God, then we become freer to trust others, to forgive them when they fail, and to continue claiming his grace and mercy for ourselves and extending them to those around us.

A foundation of trust makes communities into what I like to call safety zones—in contrast to the danger zones where construction is underway or explosives are being detonated. I believe that in order for heart-to-heart communication to take place, people must feel safe. And community becomes safe because of our attitudes toward others and the ways we choose to communicate. Ideally, the church should be the safest of places, where people can be transparent about who they are and what they need. Unfortunately, the church has often been a place where people feel judged and excluded.

In order to have their communities be safety zones for its members, I encourage folks to become good listeners. This means that we leave the judgments to the Lord and try to focus on the real messages being conveyed by other people. Whether physical (food or transportation), emotional (comfort or compassion), or spiritual (prayer support and counseling) needs are being shared, we need to tune in to others in ways that make them feel comfortable with us.

At the same time, there will be occasions when we are called to speak truths that may not be well received, and those times require discernment, wisdom, and courage on our parts. Speaking truth to one another is probably one of the greatest catalysts to personal and community growth. Even if the truth is painful to speak or to hear, it usually produces the fruits of respect, clarity, and cooperation.

As we've seen throughout David's life, God often used his prophets to communicate his messages. First, Samuel sought out David and anointed him as God's king for the nation of Israel. Then Nathan used a parable to sneak up on David and speak the truth regarding his affair with Bathsheba and the murder of her husband. God also used Nathan to tell David about the consequences of those actions. Although David undoubtedly didn't enjoy hearing what Nathan had to say, his hearing that truth was crucial to changing his heart attitude and returning to God. Hearing the hard truth from one we trust is often what it takes for us to change as well.

Finally, one of the most basic but overlooked factors in effective communication is simply consistency. If we don't practice open conversation on an ongoing basis, it's easy for uncertainty and second-guessing to morph into bitterness and grudges. Without regular dialogues, our human insecurities can work overtime and read into the behaviors and silences of others things that aren't there at all.

Effective community growth relies on freedom of speech, but we know that honest communication doesn't always come easily. We have to work to find ways to keep the channels open, making sure that communication is an exchange and not just a monologue where one person is preaching to the other. Bottom line, we need to establish trust, ensure safety, and be consistent in our communication.

## AGAINST THE GRAIN

Open, trusting communication certainly reduces the chances for conflict, but sooner or later problems will arise that honest communication alone can't solve. Instead, what's required then is understanding, compassion, and—the third wheel on our community wagon—forgiveness.

Learning to forgive and to ask for forgiveness is a more challenging task than the other components involved in building community. In some ways, forgiveness goes against the grain of everything we feel, particularly our sense of justice. When people wrong us, we want them to realize what they've done, own it, apologize, and make up for the loss. And when we wrong people, our selfish human nature kicks in. We usually feel justified doing what we did, and we struggle to swallow our pride and ask for forgiveness.

King David faced a tough forgiveness assignment. He was forced to wrestle with forgiving someone he loved who had betrayed him—his own son Absalom. The story sounds like an episode of *All My Children* or some other soap opera because the events are so tragic and so unvarnished in their revelation of some base human emotions.

The saga began when David's son Amnon became infatuated with his half-sister Tamar. Pretending to be sick, Amnon requested Tamar's presence and her home cooking to help him feel better. When he revealed his passion for her, Tamar rightfully wanted no part of such a relationship and tried to flee. Amnon, however, acted on his lust and anger at being rejected and raped his sister (see 2 Samuel 13).

The story didn't end there. Tamar took solace in the house of her big brother Absalom, who was naturally enraged when he learned what Amnon had done. David, too, was furious when he discovered what had happened, for he himself had instructed Tamar to nurse Amnon, unaware of his son's ruse. Perhaps if forgiveness had entered the story at this point, many lives could have been spared and David's legacy less tarnished. Yet forgiveness didn't even seem to be on anyone's radar screen.

Absalom harbored a grudge and seized an opportunity two years later to have his brother murdered. During the celebration after the sheepshearing, Absalom had Amnon killed and then ran away to avoid their father's wrath. After some time, Absalom returned to Jerusalem and, with the help of

David's friend and general, Joab, reunited with his father. "Then the king summoned Absalom, and he came in and bowed down with his face to the ground before the king. And the king kissed Absalom" (2 Samuel 14:33). Here was another clear opportunity for some honest communication and forgiveness to occur. And David seemed willing.

Absalom, on the other hand, resented having to humble himself before his father and king. Right before the reunion, Absalom told Joab, "Now then, I want to see the king's face, and if I am guilty of anything, let him put me to death" (2 Samuel 14:32). Apparently Absalom felt justified in his past actions. So, despite his reunion with David, Absalom's ambition and selfish nature set the course for a bitter struggle between father and son.

Absalom set himself up outside the city gates and intercepted people from the outlying areas who were coming to see the king to solve a problem:

> Then Absalom would say to [the traveler], "Look, your claims are valid and proper, but there is no representative of the king to hear you." And Absalom would add, "If only I were appointed judge in the land! Then everyone who has a complaint or case could come to me and I would see that he gets justice."
>
> Also, whenever anyone approached him to bow down before him, Absalom would reach out his hand, take hold of him and kiss him. Absalom behaved in this way toward all the Israelites who came to the king asking for justice, and so he stole the hearts of the men of Israel. (2 Samuel 15:3–6)

And we think our politicians are crafty! Absalom could definitely hold his own with the best of them! Conniving and manipulating and thereby turning his father's loyal subjects into rebels—there's a certain brilliance to

Absalom's wicked plan. By creating a problem in people's minds ("there is no representative of the king to hear you"), he simultaneously discredited David's authority as well as set himself up as the solution. This very strategy continues today, tearing apart families, churches, and business communities. Like Absalom, a gifted individual gets so caught up in her own agenda and committed to its execution that she ignores the cost to her community.

Such a selfish pursuit contrasts sharply with David's reaction to his son's full-scale attempt to seize the throne. After fleeing the city and Absalom's forces, and several skirmishes later, David faced the final showdown. He divided his army into three flanks and prepared to wage war against his own son. In the midst of this, we see a small but quite significant act:

> The king told the troops, "I myself will surely march out with you."
>
> But the men said, "You must not go out; if we are forced to flee, they won't care about us. Even if half of us die, they won't care; but you are worth ten thousand of us. It would be better now for you to give us support from the city."
>
> The king answered, "I will do whatever seems best to you."
>
> So the king stood beside the gate while all the men marched out in units of hundreds and of thousands. (2 Samuel 18:2–5)

I find this scene significant for several reasons. Foremost, it's striking that David was willing to fight his son in the first place. Even if he had been willing to confront Absalom at the palace, David had apparently realized that he must choose the course of action that was best for the nation, not his own pride. But I know that some fathers might rather be killed by their own sons than to wage war against them. However, in order to keep his nation united, in order to preserve what he had—with the Lord's help—

worked so hard to build, David had to do the unthinkable and square off against his own flesh and blood.

The other reason this little scene resonates is because we see in David the exact opposite of Absalom's selfish behavior. Specifically, we see David sacrifice his desire to fight alongside his men and agree to stay away from the front line. David was willing to listen to his community and to act according to their counsel even though their desire ran counter to his personal preference. His son, on the other hand, consistently abandoned what was best for the community and remained stubbornly fixated on his own personal goal.

The story did not end happily. In the midst of this battle, Absalom was killed—and, amazingly, the king was devastated. Despite the incredible turmoil and heartache that his son had caused him as well as the nation, David grieved the loss particularly deeply. I can't help but wonder if the loss was made more painful because David saw himself in his son's passion, drive, and giftedness. Or perhaps David realized that the nature of forgiveness is undermined when we place our own agendas above the good of our community, when we are determined to follow our own paths regardless of the costs.

## FOUR SEASONS

Trusting, communicating, forgiving—these are key to building and sustaining community, and since these three wheels require ongoing attention, ending our discussion with some thoughts on perseverance seems fitting. Each of these wheels requires everyone's commitment for the long term if the community is to grow stronger. If we get burned by people in our community, if we feel misunderstood, or if we harbor grudges, then we will not enjoy the benefits of living in community or live to our full potentials.

So we must continue to invest in the people around us, serving them, receiving from them, and letting God use those experiences to grow us into communities that create results and change lives for the better. *We must recognize that significance occurs within the day-in, day-out process of interacting with others.* Just as we make changes in our gardens according to the seasons of the year, so we must adapt to changes within our communities as they struggle, grow, get pruned, grow some more, and flourish. When the harsh circumstances of winter come, for instance, we must huddle together (like the penguins!) in order to sustain one another. When the spring and summer months provide us the opportunities, we must share in the work of planting and nourishing. And when it's time for the harvest, we must be willing to serve and celebrate all that God has done and is doing.

Clearly, perseverance requires a commitment to a larger purpose than our own personal goals and dreams. In order for our community wagon to roll along smoothly, we can't overlook this fourth wheel. Perseverance enables us to bear one another's burdens for the long haul and to experience the fullness of joyful lives. Perseverance also allows us to enjoy the journey, even when the road is bumpy, knowing that we're fulfilling our purposes in community.

# CHAPTER 15

## *Lifetime Achievement*

One of my all-time favorite films is the classic *Citizen Kane*. You might recall that it deals with the story of multimillionaire Charles Foster Kane, a character loosely based on the real-life newspaper tycoon William Randolph Hearst. The movie begins with Kane's dying word—"Rosebud"—and follows a reporter named Thompson as he searches to uncover the meaning of this cryptic final message.

As Thompson explores Kane's life, he discovers the story of a boy who was basically abandoned by his family when gold was discovered on their Colorado property. Raised by guardians and investment bankers, Kane struggled to find his place in life despite his vast wealth. His first marriage to a prominent woman from a high-profile family ended in divorce. After dabbling in the newspaper business, Kane ran for political office but was blackmailed into dropping out of the race. He devoted the rest of his life to collecting: first another wife, then other businesses, then objects of art, a menagerie of wild animals, and all of the very best things of life. Nonetheless, for all his accumulated wealth and fancy possessions, Kane died a lonely, isolated, sad man.

Perhaps one of the reasons I enjoy this film is that it parallels with the message of Ecclesiastes. Like a modern-day Solomon, Charlie Kane had everything, yet he came to realize that he had nothing. His sprawling estate was dismantled to pay taxes. The single word "Rosebud" referred to the only happy time in his childhood. He had cut himself off from the people who had tried to love him—his first wife, his son, his best friend, and his second wife. Kane's story is a cautionary tale that remains as relevant today as it did half a century ago when it was filmed.

## MADE FOR MORE

*Citizen Kane* remains relevant because so many of us still strive to find our identities and significance in wealth, power, and relationships with the opposite sex—none of which can provide fulfillment. In fact, I'll never forget the words of a college friend of mine. He and I ran into each other at a class reunion and began catching up. I could tell from his references to his work and travels that he had done very well for himself and was enjoying great success. As he began asking about my ministry and me, though, our conversation went to a deeper level.

Finally, my friend looked at me and said, "You know, Jim, I think that one of the reasons the Lord has blessed me so much is to show me that none of the blessings are enough. I love my job, but it doesn't fill the hole in my heart. My wife is the most wonderful woman I could ever imagine loving, but I still get lonely. I have great kids and more money than I'll spend in this lifetime. But lately, as I've gotten older, I've come to realize that I was made for more."

My classmate's observation is something I believe we all feel at a deep level. We want more than just a lifetime achievement award at the end of our lives. Yet we still see so many Citizen Kanes around us, those celebrities, tycoons, and millionaires who achieve their wildest dreams only to realize they're still unsatisfied. That dissatisfaction comes because, ultimately, our cravings for significance are a spiritual hunger. We long to know God and experience his love and grace. Yet even after we're committed to him and to following Jesus, we still may find ourselves wondering why we're on this planet. That's why we must embrace the fullness of who God made us to be and then serve others using the gifts he's given us. In essence, that pursuit is what this book is all about.

As I've interacted with numerous people about living a meaningful life, I've seen that one of the most telling benchmarks of a person's significance is the impact he or she has on the community. Sometimes this is easy to evaluate in the present. We simply point to various acts of service or the quality of the relationships the person enjoys with those in the community. But what about on a larger scale? How do we know what we'll leave behind after we pass from this earth?

Considering what we'll leave behind after we die may seem a little morbid. But considering the legacy we want to pass along to those we care about most can be an incredible motivator in the present. *While it's gratifying to know that we're living in harmony with our God-given purposes, it is even more fulfilling to know that what we're doing will echo through eternity.* Our decisions and actions today aren't just about fulfilling our potential in the present. Just as the light of a star billions of miles away travels to earth, our legacies will shine on into the future.

Whenever I make this comparison, some people will tell me that they aren't that important and that while their lives matter to God and to certain individuals, they don't feel like what they're doing really shines. I think this attitude arises in part because of what we expect a lasting impact to look like. Typically, words like *legacy* and *inheritance* probably make us think of large mansions, trust funds with lots of zeros, new wings of hospitals and churches, and elaborate tombstones and monuments. But in our hearts we know that these tangible items are not what determine the legacy of a significant life.

That's why I believe we must consider three areas when we're assessing the significance of someone's life. Certainly, we can't judge people's lives and the hidden motives of their hearts. Only God knows those things. But we can evaluate the fruit of a person's life and how that fruit serves as a testimony to the past, a provision for the present, and a promise for the future. In order to illustrate what I mean, let me take you to a special place.

## The Tree of Life

When I was a boy, one of my favorite places to visit was my grandparents' small farm in rural Pennsylvania. I loved the animals, the many experiences I had in God's creation, and the lessons for life that I learned there. The setting for one lesson that has always stuck with me came from the big, century-old apple tree near the barn. Before I heard the biblical concept that we are known by our fruit, it was instilled in me by my mother.

I remember standing with her under that tree one beautiful sunny day in early fall. Apples dotted the ground around us, and we were there to find some of the best ones to turn into a pie. As I looked for the perfect apples, my mother called me over and directed me to look carefully at the trunk. "Do you have any idea how old this tree is?" she asked.

I shook my head as I stared up at the branches that seemed to reach up to heaven.

"If we were to cut through the trunk of this tree and count its rings, we'd count well past one hundred. That means the tree has deep, deep roots, but even though it's old, it still produces the sweetest fruit. It's also responsible for at least a dozen of these smaller trees around it."

I plucked a pink-turning-red apple from the tree and took a big bite to see if it really was the sweetest. The flavor was sweet and tart and so delicious.

My mother smiled at my taste test and said, "That's how you know if a tree is a real life-giver—if it endured the harsh winters and summer storms of the past, if it can still provide sweet fruit in the present, and if it has produced seeds for the future. Not a bad measure of a person's life either."

I still think of my mother's words and that old apple tree every time I read Jesus's words from John's gospel:

> I am the vine; you are the branches. If a man remains in me
> and I in him, he will bear much fruit; apart from me you can
> do nothing. If anyone does not remain in me, he is like a
> branch that is thrown away and withers; such branches are
> picked up, thrown into the fire and burned. If you remain in
> me and my words remain in you, ask whatever you wish, and
> it will be given you. This is to my Father's glory, that you
> bear much fruit, showing yourselves to be my disciples.
> (John 15:5–8)

The fruit you and I bear definitely serve as good barometers of our significance. I like this symbol for measuring our eternal impact because it encompasses more than just the tangible legacy we leave behind. You see, I believe that a life of significance stands as a monument to God's goodness and faithfulness amidst the obstacles that the person overcame. As we persevere and exercise faith in the face of adversity, we become witnesses of God's character and mercy to those around us.

Being "more than conquerors" who are witnesses to others is part of a significant legacy and serves as a trophy for the suffering we endure. Because "we know that in all things God works for the good of those who love him," we are able to face the staggering losses and heartbreaking setbacks that life throws at us. When the biopsy reports are not what we hoped for, when relationships bring painful rejections, when our kids suffer, when we lose our jobs, then we discover what we're really made of. During the trials of life, we have the opportunity to become overcomers, demonstrating how wise and loving God is. (See Romans 8:28–39.)

## Go the Distance

He looks like an average guy, but my friend Rob is an Ironman triathlete. Now, I love sports and enjoyed playing baseball in college, but folks like Rob who compete in triathlons really amaze me. Some of you may be triathletes yourself, but for those of you—like me—who aren't, a triathlon is a three-part competition in which people swim, bike, and run. The different levels of the sport mean different distances for each leg. The Ironman swim is over two miles in open water, the bike ride is over a hundred miles, and the athletes finish by running a marathon—all in one day!

When I asked Rob how he did it, he just shrugged and said, "If I can do it, anyone can. You just have to put your mind to it and then be disciplined about the training so that your body holds up over the long haul." He often quoted phrases like, "Go the distance," pointing out the huge role really believing this adage plays. "It's a reminder," he said, "that it's an endurance race and that you only win if you finish."

I like Rob's attitude about what it takes to endure the grueling training for the big event. It's the same kind of endurance we need in our spiritual lives if we are to leave legacies of real substance for our communities. You see, people like Rob inspire all of us to go the distance and stay in the race of life for the long haul. In fact, this is a role we are all called to fulfill. The apostle Paul knew the importance of endurance and its role in leaving a significant legacy:

> Do you not know that in a race all the runners run, but only
> one gets the prize? Run in such a way as to get the prize.
> Everyone who competes in the games goes into strict training.
> They do it to get a crown that will not last; but we do it to
> get a crown that will last forever. (1 Corinthians 9:24–25)

If we are to leave enduring legacies, then we must demonstrate an Ironman's determination to stay in the race and do what it takes to finish well. In terms of our apple tree metaphor, such a commitment to survival and overcoming produces a hardy trunk with many rings, deep roots, and strong branches. As we see God provide for us, comfort us, and sustain us, we grow in our faith, and that growth in turn encourages and inspires others as they face their own hardships. One significant life can touch so many people, and that fact is one more reason why we can only live significantly in community.

## FRESH FRUIT

Besides offering a testimony to God's faithfulness in the past, a significant legacy is also known by the quality of its present fruit. In other words, not only does our past demonstrate our endurance and serve as a testament to God's glory, but our fruit, when it remains fresh, nourishes our community members after we're gone. An apple tree can endure the harshest storms for decades, but if it produces tiny sour apples, then it really hasn't accomplished much. With God's guidance, we can let this concept of fresh fruit inform our decisions about what to pour our energies and resources into in this life. We must ask ourselves, *Does what I'm doing benefit only me in the moment, or will it serve others for eternity?*

While this may be an easy question to answer in theory, the answer is one of the hardest to practice day to day. And that's all the more reason for us to stay focused on more than our immediate gratification. This assignment can be really tough to live out in our present society where we're bombarded with the message that if we only consume the latest product, we can feel great right now—or at least until the credit-card bill comes in!

Although this challenge to deny ourselves instant gratification may be compounded by our culture's consumerism, the issue itself is nothing new. David certainly struggled with knowing where to direct his energies and talents, and we've seen that when he followed God and served others, significance emerged. When David followed his whims and served his appetites and fears, chaos followed.

In the end, however, David knew what it meant to live a significant life, and that's evident in the legacy he left behind, a legacy that continues to this day. Let me explain.

On a recent tour of Israel, I asked our guide about Israel's greatest season of prosperity under the reign of Solomon. I assumed that Solomon's splendor must have been the proudest moment of Israel's long history. The guide said, "No. David is the most esteemed, admired king in Israel." When David came to power, he explained, the people had nothing; when he left, they had plenty. When David started as king, Israel was only six thousand square miles; by the end of his reign, it was sixty thousand.

But the issue is not about bigger being better. Rather, the increase in Israel's size was the by-product, or fruit, of one man fulfilling his God-given purpose. In the case of the nation of Israel, wealth and prosperity were nothing compared to the restoration of dignity. While it's tempting to measure success by material gain, for the Israelites success was about becoming a people shaped in the image of God. May that be our measure of success as well as we focus on fulfilling our purposes, knowing that God will preserve well into the future the good fruit we produce and use it to provide a foundation of righteousness and blessing for those who knew us.

## BACK TO THE FUTURE

In addition to the testimony of the past and the fruit of the present, a significant legacy looks ahead and casts a long shadow into future generations. People who produce this kind of forward fruit pursue a vision larger than their own and commit themselves to working with others to accomplish mighty goals. Anticipating future needs but also acting on faith, they plant seeds wherever they go, and they know that God can take our mustard seeds of faith and move mountains.

And we definitely see in David's legacy its impact on the future. Consider especially the psalms he composed and their impact on people of God for generations after the songwriter-shepherd's death. I love the way those poems so beautifully express both the truth of what it means to be human as well as the truth of God's character. Keeping in mind all that David experienced—from his anointing by Samuel up through another war with the Philistines after Absalom's death—read the following psalm that he composed toward the end of his life:

> The LORD is my rock, my fortress and my deliverer;
>> my God is my rock, in whom I take refuge,
>> my shield and the horn of my salvation.
> He is my stronghold, my refuge and my savior—
>> from violent men you save me.
> I call to the LORD, who is worthy of praise,
>> and I am saved from my enemies. (2 Samuel 22:2–4)

Over the course of a lifetime, David learned how to endure, and as a result he passed down a legacy to generations of people that he couldn't even imagine. He knew God's protection and faithfulness firsthand, and he wanted others to know them too. And, as I shared at the beginning of this book, one of the reasons I like David and chose him as our anchor man for living significant lives is because he was a person just like the rest of us. He came from humble beginnings, an unlikely candidate for hero and king of Israel. He was a man after God's own heart, yet flawed by his own desires. He knew what it meant to rely on God and God alone, and he knew what it meant to turn from him and hide in the darkness of his own mistakes.

In the legacy of his life—and as illustrated in this psalm—David demonstrated several characteristics of timeless fruit. First, he taught us about honor and humility. Throughout his life, David said, "I know why

I'm who I am, and I never want anyone to forget that my empowerment comes from God." As he expressed this truth in Psalm 139, "For you created my inmost being; you knit me together in my mother's womb. I praise you because I am fearfully and wonderfully made; your works are wonderful, I know that full well" (verses 13–14).

David also showed us the value of responsibility—both in the times he took charge as well as the times he made mistakes. Repeatedly as king, he failed and had to face consequences that affected his entire community. Nevertheless, God still expected the Israelites to respect their king because of his divine authority. David reminded us that our legacies have far less to do with relying on ourselves and far more to do with obeying God.

Finally, the life of David showed us what it means to glorify God through praise and thanksgiving. As one of the most gifted poets of all time, David consistently urged us to remember our source of blessing, even when our circumstances are grim. Whether we've blown it and need to ask forgiveness (see Psalm 51), or feel depressed and surrounded by our enemies (see Psalm 27), or feel overwhelmed by the bounty of God's goodness (see Psalm 21)—in every situation David directs us back to our only constant in life, our Rock. I remain convinced that this kind of legacy, directed back to the Source from which we were created, endures forever.

## GRACE AND GODSPEED

David showed us that no life is perfect, that every life contains broken places, but that God's faithfulness sustains us. Our lives are never wasted when we seek God first and willingly serve him and the people he places around us. Every life really does impact another...for better or worse.

My prayer for this book is that it will challenge you to take ownership of your life as never before and that it will inspire you to make a difference in the community where God has placed you. *There is no one-size-fits-all perfect formula for living a significant life. The key is faith that God honors his word and delights in empowering his children—you and me—to be all that we can be.*

And, as we come to the end of this book, my prayer for you is that you will fully embrace who you are and how God has made you. My hope is that you will become a sturdy tree of life, thriving despite adversity, blooming with delicious fruit, and planting seeds for future harvests. My vision is that you would stand surrounded by a vast forest of other life-giving trees and together form a formidable community that will demonstrate the love of Christ and power of God as never before. Finally, on this journey of significance, I wish you grace and Godspeed as you discover the joy and peace that can only come from fulfilling your eternal potential every day of your life.

To learn more about WaterBrook Press and view
our catalog of products, log on to our Web site:
**www.waterbrookpress.com**

WATERBROOK
PRESS